Managing

the

Devolved

Budget

Managing
the
Devolved
Budget

Essential skills for the public sector

Jennifer Bean
Lascelles Hussey

PUBLICATIONS

HB PUBLICATIONS
(Incorporated as Givegood Limited)

Published by

HB Publications
London, England

British Library Cataloguing in Publication Data
Reprinted 1998

ISBN 1 899448 01 2

Printed and bound in Great Britain by
JRDigital Print Services Ltd, Whitstable, KENT

Contents

Chapter 1

INTRODUCTION

The control of public sector finances has increasingly become a key issue for scrutiny by Government. In response, the public sector has had to take a positive approach to implementing successful systems for financial management and control. Devolving budgetary responsibility has therefore become a commonly adopted method for achieving the effective control of financial resources.

Managing the Devolved Budget has been developed to meet the needs of those working in public sector environments such as central government; local and regional authorities; health authorities; police authorities; educational institutions, and so on. The text is particularly relevant as many public sector employees have now been given some form of budgetary responsibility. This is often a new area of activity and requires them to have a certain level of financial skill.

The publication has been designed as a text which can be used for reference and act as an important part of a managers own personal development. At the conclusion of each chapter is a series of exercises which encourage the reader to focus on the key issues covered. Suggested solutions to the exercises are provided in the final section.

Managing The Devolved Budget is presented in a simple format which is easy to read and makes practical sense. It will give those who have any form of budgetary responsibility an understanding of the process behind budget setting and control and will provide tools with which they can undertake these tasks with greater awareness and confidence.

It is recognised that many budget holders work within constraints. This may be with respect to policies, limited resources, limited support, and restricted access to financial experts. Although circumstances may not be perfect, ideas are given within the text which will enable the most common constraints to be taken into account whilst allowing the budget holder to achieve the objective of controlling a budget.

The task of financial management and control is now relevant to many job descriptions in the public sector. For those who may wish to pursue a career within public service, this book will highlight the type of knowledge and skill now required to be fully prepared for acquiring budgetary responsibilities.

Whilst demand for public services increase and expectations of quality rise, there is increasing pressure on publicly funded organisations to be accountable and achieve value for money. The devolvement of budgets has been a common step forward to meeting these challenges.

Chapter 2

DEVOLVING THE BUDGET

What is Devolvement?

It is necessary to firstly clarify the meaning of devolvement as this term carries many interpretations and definitions. For the purpose of this text we will be using the following definition.

Devolvement is:

> *the process whereby budgets are devolved to an individual who becomes the budget holder and who will be totally responsible and accountable for that budget. Ideally management and financial responsibilities are aligned such that the budget holder is accountable for the financial implications of his/her management decisions.*

Other terms that are often used interchangeably with devolvement are "delegation" and "decentralisation". Both these activities usually take place as part of the process of devolvement. Usually budgets are firstly decentralised, then devolved, and then sometimes delegated. In order to understand these terms more clearly, the definitions of delegation and decentralisation for the purpose of this text are given below:

Decentralisation is:

> *where the control of budgets is dis-aggregated from the centre and allocated to other areas of the organisation such as departments, divisions, branches etc.*

Delegation is:

> *where budgets are delegated to nominated budget holders who are responsible for <u>monitoring</u> the budget, but are not accountable for the budget as they will have little or no control over its construction and its usage.*

There are some common factors that apply to all three terms:

❖ They all involve a transfer of financial control to some degree away from a central point

❖ They all result in finance being more closely linked to service delivery or activity

❖ They all result in a spreading of financial responsibilities throughout the organisation

In order to further appreciate the difference between each of the three terms it is helpful to illustrate the normal devolvement process by way of the following chart:

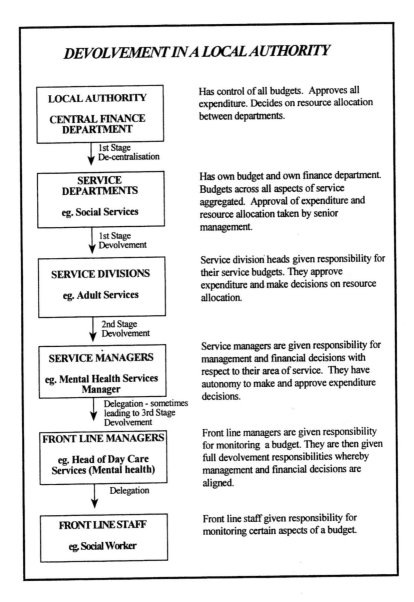

DEVOLVEMENT IN A LOCAL AUTHORITY

LOCAL AUTHORITY

CENTRAL FINANCE DEPARTMENT

Has control of all budgets. Approves all expenditure. Decides on resource allocation between departments.

1st Stage De-centralisation

SERVICE DEPARTMENTS

eg. Social Services

Has own budget and own finance department. Budgets across all aspects of service aggregated. Approval of expenditure and resource allocation taken by senior management.

1st Stage Devolvement

SERVICE DIVISIONS

eg. Adult Services

Service division heads given responsibility for their service budgets. They approve expenditure and make decisions on resource allocation.

2nd Stage Devolvement

SERVICE MANAGERS

eg. Mental Health Services Manager

Service managers are given responsibility for management and financial decisions with respect to their area of service. They have autonomy to make and approve expenditure decisions.

Delegation - sometimes leading to 3rd Stage Devolvement

FRONT LINE MANAGERS

eg. Head of Day Care Services (Mental health)

Front line managers are given responsibility for monitoring a budget. They are then given full devolvement responsibilities whereby management and financial decisions are aligned.

Delegation

FRONT LINE STAFF

eg. Social Worker

Front line staff given responsibility for monitoring certain aspects of a budget.

Diagram 1

Why Devolve Budgets?

There are a number of advantages to be gained from devolving a budget, some of which are summarised as follows:

❖ Managers and officers who are involved with the direct delivery of a service understand service requirements, and are therefore in the best position to target financial resources efficiently and effectively to the benefit of the end user.

❖ There is greater incentive for budget holders to maximise value for money if they consider they have real control over financial resources and can reap benefits from the efficient and effective use of the budget.

❖ Greater effort may be put into budget monitoring and control as there are usually more people involved in the budgetary process as a result of devolvement.

❖ Decisions can be made more quickly if the budget holder responsible for the service can also authorise the use of resources. The budget holder is in a position to exploit opportunities and avoid problems by being in control of the budget.

❖ The budget holder can be held accountable for their decisions, and made to take responsibility for their actions. The impact of management decisions on financial resources can be effectively measured and assessed.

There are also a number of dis-advantages that need to be taken into account when embarking on a devolvement strategy. These include:

- ❖ Devolvement often requires the person who becomes the budget holder to undertake additional duties including budgetary monitoring and control activities. These areas may not be part of the individual's job description and will often be an area for which no prior training has been given. Certain budget holders neither have the skill or aptitude for this new task and no desire to acquire it.

- ❖ Devolvement requires the organisation to give autonomy to staff lower down the hierarchy and hence removes some control away from senior management. This may leave senior managers feeling vulnerable if they lack confidence in less senior staff.

- ❖ Devolvement means that the managers who become budget holders have to take account of the financial consequences of their decisions. This may lead to a conflict of interest in making what would be a "professionally correct" decision but not necessarily a "financially viable" one.

Most of the dis-advantages of devolvement may be overcome by undertaking the following activities as part of the devolvement process:

- ❖ Ensuring that staff gain a thorough understanding of the meaning and process of devolvement and what their budgetary responsibilities will be in advance of them receiving devolved responsibility.

❖ Ensuring that the organisation has established clear guidelines with respect to how devolvement is going to work. This is achieved by stating where the budget holder's responsibilities begin and end.

❖ Ensuring that clear service objectives, priorities, and guidelines, are set so that the budget holder knows how to balance professionalism with respect to service delivery and the new financial responsibilities they hold.

❖ Establishing clarity with respect to budgetary responsibility by appointing one budget holder for each budget. This will ensure that there is no misunderstanding with respect to who is responsible for what.

❖ Ensuring that budget holders receive sufficient support from senior managers and finance officers to enable them to undertake their role in an effective and efficient manner for the benefit of the whole organisation.

Making managers more responsible and accountable for their decisions in financial terms has its benefits, however, achieving the benefit will be dependent on taking a practical approach to devolvement. Hence, devolvement should only occur when due consideration has been given to a range of factors such as the size of budget and the type of budget to be devolved.

The Devolvement Process

The steps in the process may be summarised as follows:

❖ Decentralise

❖ Identify appropriate budgets for devolvement

❖ Identify potential budget holders

❖ Provide training and support for budget holders

❖ Ensure budget holders are aware of the service objectives to be achieved with the devolved budgets

❖ Ensure budget holders have the appropriate resources needed to monitor and control budgets, including access to information, Information Technology (IT), administrative staff, and so on

❖ Provide budget holders with real autonomy and flexibility to make decisions with respect to expenditure and service delivery

Commonly Devolved Budgets

Some of the most commonly devolved budgets are highlighted on the next pages:

Salaries

This budget is one of the most contentious budgets when it comes to devolvement. Salaries tend to be the largest revenue expenditure budget for most public sector organisations, normally representing over half of overall spending. Hence, devolvement to an appropriate level may assist with control and monitoring of this important budget. Depending on the nature of the organisation and service being provided, the appropriate level of devolvement can vary from the most senior person in the hierarchy such as the Chief Executive Officer, to a frontline manager, such as the head of a day nursery.

Supplies and Services

This heading covers a whole range of different budgets. It relates to the expenditure on any item which is utilised in order to deliver the service. This may include items such as materials, stationery, and services provided by third parties. These budgets are the most obvious to devolve as they often require decision making on a day to day basis by operational staff.

Property costs

These costs include everything needed in order to run and maintain the property. They include items such as rent, rates, insurance, heat, light, repairs, maintenance, and so on. It is quite usual to devolve these areas of cost to either service managers or a service department. There may be a limit as to how much positive action the budget holder can take with respect to controlling these costs as many of them are uncontrollable, e.g. rent and rates. However, a devolved budget holder may be in a position to decide how much accommodation is required and therefore have some impact on these costs.

Internal support service costs

In many large organisations, certain activities are performed by centralised departments, or by sections within a department. These activities which typically include finance, personnel, property (in some cases), information technology, and so on, support the organisation in the delivery of its services. They are essential activities and it is often considered that decentralisation of these types of services should only occur to the extent that economies of scale are not totally lost. It has been common practice to allocate the cost of supporting services to those areas of the organisation that directly deliver services so that a true cost of service delivery can be established. When budgets for support services are devolved to service managers, there is often very little control that can be exercised by the budget holder. This is because the support service budget is usually allocated on an arbitrary basis and remains fixed for the year. Devolved budgets for these areas are only controllable if an internal market exists and budget holders have the power to decide on the quality or quantity of service that is required.

Capital Expenditure

Capital expenditure represents expenditure on items that have an ongoing value to the organisation. These items are often referred to as fixed assets in accounting terms and include land, buildings, furniture, fixtures, fittings, equipment, and so on. The sort of budget that tends to be devolved in this area is the purchase of furniture and equipment which can easily be controlled by the budget holder. Major works projects, such as building work, are often handled by a specialist (and sometimes central) department.

Income

Where a service generates income from fees or charges, the responsibility for controlling the income may readily be devolved to operational staff. An example would be in the case of a leisure centre where entrance and membership fees are charged for a range of different activities. The centre manager would have devolved responsibility to ensure that fee income meets the budgeted income targets.

Level of Devolvement

A school of thought exists which states that budgets should be devolved to the lowest possible tier within an organisation. This allows the control of spending to be as near to the direct provision of services as possible. For example, in a hospital, certain operational budgets could be devolved to the ward sister, or, in a school to a teacher, and so on. Devolvement should ideally be to the staff member who makes the spending decision and authorises the expenditure.

Common sense dictates that at certain levels, devolvement may become inefficient and difficult to operate. It is therefore important to consider the following factors when deciding on an appropriate level of devolvement:

❖   Size of organisation

❖   Type of structure

❖   Type of budget

❖   Controllability of budget

❖   Size of budget

We discuss each of these issues in the following paragraphs.

Size of Organisation

The size of organisation is very important to the level of devolvement. Larger organisations often require a greater level of devolvement to ensure that financial monitoring and control is more closely aligned with the point of service delivery. For example, the budget for materials may be devolved to heads of departments or below in a large further education college, whereas it may not be devolved below the head teacher in a small primary school.

Type of Structure

The organisational structure very often dictates where decisions are made. Usually a public sector organisation has a clear hierarchical structure where key decisions, particularly financial ones, are often taken at the top of the hierarchy. The more levels within the hierarchy, the greater the number of stages in the devolvement process. In a very hierarchical structure, devolvement may not go down to the same level as it would within an organisation with a flatter structure and fewer management tiers.

Type of Budget

The type of budget has an impact on devolvement. For example, a budget for travel expenses may be devolved down to probation officer level whereas a budget for property costs may only be devolved to cost centre level. The reason for this is that it is not always practical to divide shared overheads such as property costs between individuals for control purposes. In contrast, budgets for items such as travel expenses can be easily identified and devolved to an individual officer for control.

Controllability of Budget

Some budgets are uncontrollable. For example, both central and local government will have statutory responsibilities that have to be met, such as spending in respect to homelessness, health and safety issues, etc. Such service areas have to be provided irrespective of the budget allocation. This makes the budget difficult to control and hence devolvement to lower levels within the organisation may be impractical.

Size of Budget

Devolving a budget below a certain level can become unworkable depending on the amounts concerned. For example, to devolve a furniture budget to each individual member of staff may lead to the amounts being devolved being too small to buy any one item of furniture. These budgets would normally be held at a higher level and expenditure targeted strategically to meet the furniture needs of the whole office. This requires an individual to be responsible for furniture purchasing decisions and the furniture budget for the office.

Being Responsible for a Devolved Budget

A budget holder should be responsible for all aspects of the budget. This includes setting, monitoring and controlling the budget. In order to be effective in this role, the budget holder has to:

❖ Become involved with setting the budget in the first instance (although this may not always be possible in the first year of devolvement)

❖ Be given a certain amount of autonomy to make financial decisions and to amend budgets part way through the year as required

❖ Take responsibility if things do not go according to plan

❖ Have support to make decisions through an effective financial and management information system

The following chapters in the book will help prepare the budget holder to be as effective as possible in his/her role.

SUMMARY

☐ Devolvement is usually most relevant to large organisations carrying out a range of different activities

☐ In practice, devolvement of budgets will vary from one type of public sector organisation to another

☐ Organisations should carefully embark on the process of devolvement such that budget holders are prepared for their new roles

☐ All types of budgets may be devolved, but common sense should ensure that the level of devolvement is appropriate given the type of service and the type of budget

☐ Devolvement should result in management and financial decision making being aligned

Exercise 1
Devolvement in Practice

You are given the following scenario:

Blackstone Leisure Centre (BLC) has recently been subject to competitive tendering. Three of the existing managers of the Centre decided to come together independently and put in a private bid for BLC in which they were successful. Having won the tender they now wish to implement devolved budgetary responsibility. Having attended a number of finance courses they are now confused as to how to go about the process. The current situation is described as follows:

The three managers who came together to bid for the Centre were the Head of Activities, the Head of Finance and the Head of Repairs, Maintenance and Operations. They have now taken different roles as Centre Director and two Centre Managers and new personnel were appointed to their old posts. Their new responsibilities involve overall responsibility for BLC. Due to the long opening hours it is necessary for shift working and they wish to ensure that there is always a Centre Manager on site. There are a total of four areas of operation, these are called service areas, each of which has a Head. The service areas are as follows:

Activities

This includes all the activities that BLC provide such as swimming pool activities, gymnasium activities, fitness classes, sports hall activities, health and beauty treatments and other ad hoc activities as demanded by the public. There are a number of key personnel which include the head swimming pool attendant, the head fitness instructor and a health and safety officer. There are 12 other permanent staff and a large number of sessional staff used for specific classes/sessions. All staff are appropriately qualified for their jobs.

Finance

This includes all finance functions, personnel functions and administration. There is a financial controller who is responsible for the day to day bookkeeping, production of reports, payroll etc. who is supported by three other staff. There is a personnel officer responsible for training, as well as all the personnel functions. This officer is supported by one assistant. In addition, there is a senior administrator who currently undertakes all the ordering of goods and services and manages two secretarial staff.

Repairs, Maintenance, and Operations

This includes responsibility for all maintenance works within the building including controlling the maintenance contracts that have been agreed for the boiler systems etc. In addition, this service area is responsible for the cleaning, reception area, external areas such as the car park, and the security. There are 15 to 25 full and part-time staff engaged in this work. Key staff include the contracts officer and the cleaning service manager.

Entertainment

This includes the provision of bar and restaurant facilities, (two main areas in the building) lettings of space to the public for weddings etc., and the arrangement of a number of events during the year, often with a view to promoting BLC. The head of entertainment is also responsible for the general marketing of the Centre including the production of brochures, press releases and so on. There are two full time staff who have key roles, these are the catering manager and the press and publicity officer. In addition, there are four other full time staff and a number of part-time and casual staff used subject to demand.

To date all the budgets had been held centrally and broken down into the following broad headings:

Expenditure
Salaries and Employee related costs
Sessional Fees
Property Costs (including utilities)
Supplies and Services
Capital Expenditure (Furniture and Equipment)
Other General Expenditure
Income
Fees and Charges for activities
Subsidies/Grants from central and local government
Fund-raising events

It is clear that each area of service requires separate budgets broken down in a way that is practical and relevant. Work has yet to be done in this area.

Given the above scenario undertake the following:

a)   Identify the level to which budgets should ideally be devolved

b)   Consider the possible problems that may occur with the ideal level of devolvement and give a practical solution.

Suggested solutions to this exercise can be found on page 135.

Exercise 2

Devolving Budgets in your Own Organisation

If relevant, consider the following questions and make notes for your own reference.

1. At present do you have a devolved budget and what does devolvement mean in your organisation?

2. Do you consider that more or fewer budgets should be devolved, and to what levels?

3. What positive changes do you think could be made to make devolvement more effective in your area of activity (always consider if the suggestions made are practical given the current environment)?

Chapter 3

SETTING THE BUDGET

What is a Budget?

A budget can be defined in a number of different ways. Popular definitions talk about an amount of money that can be spent on a particular item, or a projection of next year's income and expenditure. The definition that will be used in this text is **"a financial plan"**. This definition is important because it emphasises the need to link finance to planned activity; the financial plan has to be part of an overall plan.

The ideal way to prepare a budget is to initially begin with the objectives for the organisation by asking what is the organisation trying to achieve? This principle is relevant for private, public and voluntary organisations. Clear direction is a key to successful budget setting. When it is clear what the organisation is trying to achieve then the various departments and sections can establish their own objectives that are consistent with the overarching organisational objectives.

Business Plans

Many organisations produce business or service plans on a regular basis which set out organisational objectives and how they are to be achieved. A business plan should always be supported by a financial plan which sets out how finance will be generated and utilised over the period of the plan. The business plan is becoming a more popular tool as public sector organisations take a more "business like" approach to service delivery. The process of developing a business plan is not covered in this book, but is an ideal tool to be used as part of the budget setting process.

Budget Setting Cycle

Most public sector organisations produce an annual budget and some organisations, such as local authorities, are required by law to publish their budget. In order to ensure that a budget is created by the appropriate time each year, most organisations establish a regular cycle of activities which are communicated to all those involved in the process of creating the budget. Therefore, a "budget setting cycle" is usually published and followed each year. It is important that mangers who will be responsible for any part of the budgeting process, particularly the management of a budget, are familiar with the budget setting cycle. The cycle can be driven by either a top down or bottom up approach, or a mixture of the two. Both of these approaches are explained as follows:

Top Down Approach

The top down approach to the cycle is where the main decision making body of the organisation establishes the broad budget parameters, e.g. councillors in a local authority, school governors in a school, the trust board in a NHS trust, the management committee in a voluntary organisation. These parameters will include:

* *expenditure targets which may involve savings and cuts*

* *income strategies such as the level of charges, tax rates, grants*

* *use of reserves, whether to build or utilise them*

* *key priorities for services*

Having made these decisions, departments are set cash limited budgets within which to develop their budget proposals.

Bottom Up Approach

The bottom up approach starts with the divisions setting out their plans for the year and the amount of resources needed to achieve those plans. Within public and voluntary services this is usually a net expenditure position which will have to be funded with some type of budget allocation. This information is fed up the decision making ladder and consolidated at departmental level. At this stage, decisions on priorities have to be made to ensure that the departmental budget is realistic. Changes to budgets are referred back to those who originally set the budget to make the necessary adjustments - quite often savings.

This process is continued until the department achieves a budget that reflects the divisional plans and agreement is reached over the level of financial resources required to deliver front line services. The departments will then consolidate their budgets to produce an overall organisational budget. The funding of the budget then needs to be identified and decisions made as to whether or not to raise income by charge increases, borrowing, tax increases, use of reserves, higher demands for grant income and so on. In the bottom up approach these decisions are driven by the service needs as identified at the bottom of the organisation and not the priorities set at the top.

Most organisations will have a budget setting cycle, and the length of the cycle tends to vary depending on the size, structure and the number of levels of decision making that exist within the organisation. For example, the budget setting cycle of some local authorities stretches across the whole year, whereas in a small independent organisation the cycle may be complete within a month.

Key Elements of a Budget

Most public sector services will have a number of different income and expenditure budget headings. These will be referred to using a number of terms such as budget boxes, cost centres, etc. Even though there are many different expenditure and income headings, they are usually grouped together into core areas. These core areas include:

Employee Costs ⇨ Including salaries, oncosts, overtime, agency fees, etc.

Accommodation costs ⇨ Including rents, rates, repairs, heat, light, etc.

Transportation Costs ⇨ Including travelling expenses, vehicle maintenance, etc.

Supplies and Services ⇨ Includes all direct revenue budgets that are needed to operate the service, such as materials, professional fees, contractors fees, postage, stationery and so on.

Support Service Costs ⇨ Includes service department costs such as finance, legal, personnel, etc.

Income ⇨ Charges, fees, grants, etc.

Budget Setting Techniques

There are a number of budget setting techniques that can be applied to both expenditure and income budgets. They can be used independently, or combined depending on the nature of the budgets being set. The key techniques which will be examined are as follows:

- ***Incremental Budgeting***
- ***Zero Based Budgeting***
- ***Cash Limited Budgeting***
- ***Resource Restricted Budgeting***
- ***Activity Based Budgeting***
- ***Contingency Budgeting***

Incremental Budgeting

This technique relies on using an historic base as a starting point for budget setting. The base is usually the budget or the actual figures for the previous year, or some combination of the two. The base is then used to formulate the budget for the following year by taking each budget heading and either adding or subtracting an inflation factor from the base figures and adjusting for other known factors such as savings or approved growth.

An example of the incremental approach is shown as follows:

It is September and a nursery school is to develop a budget for next year. It's financial year runs from 1 April to 31 March. They have agreed the pay award at 4% for the following year with effect from 1 July of that year, and inflation is to be 3% for all other non pay items.

Budget Heading	Previous Year Budget Figures	Incremental Adjustments	Budget for next year
Salaries	200,000	*6,000	206,000
Food	40,000	1,200	41,200
Supplies and Services	40,000	1,200	41,200
TOTAL	**280,000**	**8,400**	**288,400**

Note: *Pay award for only 9 months of year, as only effective from 1 July

The advantages and dis-advantages of this type of budgeting technique can be summarised as follows:

Advantages
- Simple
- Quick
- Accurate if little change in activity

Dis-Advantages
- Historic
- No account taken of necessary future changes
- Assumes the base is accurate
- Compounds historic errors

Incremental budgeting is best used for certain items of expenditure which are unlikely to change from year to year. For example, when staffing remains constant, salaries can be budgeted for incrementally where the increment reflects the pay award.

Zero Based Budgeting

This approach to budget setting is most strongly recommended as it is linked to the business planning process. The zero based budget assumes that all budgets are derived from first principles and that the organisation can start with a blank piece of paper; a zero base. They are based on the objectives to be achieved for the period without necessarily referring to the past. The key steps to be taken using the zero based technique are summarised as follows:

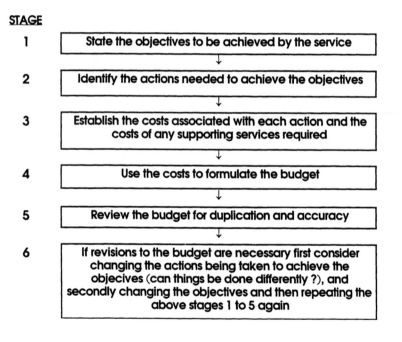

STAGE

1 — State the objectives to be achieved by the service

2 — Identify the actions needed to achieve the objectives

3 — Establish the costs associated with each action and the costs of any supporting services required

4 — Use the costs to formulate the budget

5 — Review the budget for duplication and accuracy

6 — If revisions to the budget are necessary first consider changing the actions being taken to achieve the objectives (can things be done differently ?), and secondly changing the objectives and then repeating the above stages 1 to 5 again

Diagram 2

An example of the zero based approach is given below:

> It is September and a nursery school is to develop a
> budget for next year. It's financial year runs from 1 April to
> 31 March. They have agreed that the objective for next
> year is to increase the level of nursery places available from
> 24 to 30 and to extend the range of activities offered.

Following the stages identified in diagram 2, actions needed
to achieve the objective include having to increase staff by
one additional nursery nurse; provide for 8 hours of agency
staff per week; and to purchase more play and educational
equipment to add new activities to the existing programme.
The cost of the actions are:

❖   to increase salaries to reflect the additional post;
     agency fees; in addition to increments, pay awards
     and on-costs for all staff

❖   to provide for additional purchases of the equipment
     based on estimates gained from the equipment
     suppliers

Using the information gained above a budget can then be
formulated:

Budget Heading	Budget Figures	Zero Base Assumptions
Salaries	225,800	Salaries for 10 staff plus on costs for next year £206,000 plus a nursery nurse @ £15,000 and agency fees based on 8 hrs. per week @ £12 per hour (assume a 50 week year).
Food	37,500	Cost of providing breakfast, lunch and tea for 30 children @ £5 per head per day for 50 weeks.
Supplies and Services	<u>48,000</u>	Estimates and contracts agreed for next year's supplies and services plus equipment purchases of £6,000.
TOTAL	**<u>311,300</u>**	

The advantages and dis-advantages of this type of budgeting technique can be summarised as follows:

Advantages
- Pro-active and forward looking
- Realistic and accurate
- Links into business plans

Dis-Advantages
- Time consuming
- Requires clear objectives
- Many organisations do not have a zero base as they have to work with the staff, buildings and resources they inherit from year to year

It is generally considered that the advantages of zero based budgeting outweigh the dis-advantages. Where possible, zero based principles should be adopted, even though in many cases an organisation will not have a totally zero base to begin with.

Cash Limited Budgeting

This technique is appropriate when the service area is given a set limit on its total net expenditure. It is then up to the service to identify what can be delivered within this cash limit and create a budget accordingly. This technique can be very difficult if targets on output are given without reference to the practicality of meeting those targets within a cash limit. The approach to be used in the case of cash limited budgets is to identify the costs that are fixed, i.e. those that cannot be reduced, and then to spread the balance of the budget across those items which are variable and have an element of flexibility. An example of the cash limited approach is as follows:

It is September and a nursery school is to develop a budget for next year. It's financial year runs from 1 April to 31 March. They have been given a cash limited budget of £270,000 to maintain the current level of service.

Budget Heading	Budget Figures	Cash Limit Calculations
Salaries	206,000	Salaries for 10 staff plus on costs for next year £206,000. This is a fixed cost and reflects actual salaries to be paid.
Food	24,000	Cost of providing breakfast, lunch and tea for 24 children @ £4 per head per day for 50 weeks. Expenditure reduced to the lowest possible amount for a balanced menu.
Supplies and Services	40,000	Fixed contract payments included and other expenditure reduced to fit the cash limit.
TOTAL	**270,000**	

The advantages and dis-advantages of this type of budgeting technique can be summarised as follows:

Advantages
- Clear parameters on expenditure
- Quick - negotiation limited
- Incentive to make savings to bring expenditure in line with cash limit

Dis-Advantages
- Services may have to decrease quality or quantity (or both) if cash limit insufficient
- Not linked to business objectives which may include a need for change or development
- Assumes there is sufficient flexibility in the budget to operate within a cash limit
- Inflexible - not practical for demand led/statutory services

Resource Restricted Budgeting

This type of budgeting occurs when resources to be utilised by the service are restricted. Resource restriction will be typically in respect of:

❖ Staff

❖ Equipment

❖ Property

❖ Finance (The cash limited budget is a form of resource restricted budget)

There are often many reasons why resources need to be restricted. For example, it may be necessary for the benefit of the whole organisation to set restrictions in terms of staff numbers. This action is taken as recruiting an additional full time member of staff represents an on-going commitment for the organisation and could also expose the organisation to increased redundancy costs should there be a need to reduce staff in the future. Hence, restricting the staffing resource is a common budget setting approach.

An example of the resource restricted approach is given below:

It is September and a nursery school is to develop a budget for next year. It's financial year runs from 1 April to 31 March. They have been given the following resource restrictions. Staffing establishment should not exceed 9 full time members of staff, and supplies and services expenditure should not exceed £40,000. The current level of service should be maintained.

Budget Heading	Budget Figures	Resource Restricted Calculations
Salaries	206,400	Salaries for 9 staff plus on costs for next year £185,400, plus agency fees to cover 35 hours per week @ £12 per hour for a 50 week year.
Food	30,000	Cost of providing breakfast, lunch and tea for 24 children @ £5 per head per day for 50 weeks.
Supplies and Services	40,000	Cash limited.
TOTAL	**276,400**	

The advantages and dis-advantages of this type of budgeting technique can be summarised as follows:

Advantages
- Clear parameters on expenditure
- Quick - negotiation limited
- Organisation maintains strong control over all resources

Dis-Advantages
- No consideration of the practical impact of restricting resources and the effect on services
- Not linked to business objectives which may include a need for change or development
- Inflexible - not practical for demand led/statutory services

Activity Based Budgeting

The organisation using this approach sets budgets based on the cost of providing each area of activity. If the budget has to be reduced, the organisation would examine each activity and decide which activities are to be ceased or reduced accordingly. This method of budgeting is only possible if there are clear divisions between each activity and where resources can clearly be allocated. Where resources are shared across activities (such as staff, premises, etc.) the scope for activity based budgeting is more difficult. It then relies on accurate resource allocation methods across each activity (such as charging a proportion of hours to an activity or allocating square footage).

An example of activity based budgeting is given as follows:

A nursery is about to produce an activity based budget for next year. It has identified that it delivers three key areas of service:

~ Baby room services for children less than 2 years old

~ Standard Nursery Services for children between 2 and 3 years old

~ A Nursery School Service for 4 year olds

Each activity is run by different staff and based in different parts of the nursery school building. An individual budget for each activity has been used to develop the total budget for the nursery as follows:

Budget Heading	Budget Figures	Activity Based Calculations
Baby room	85,000	Based on staff and resources utilised to provide a service for 4 children with a high staff to child ratio and lots of equipment. Apportionment is made for all shared resources such as accommodation.
Nursery	157,500	As above but for 14 children with a lower staff ratio.
Nursery School	52,500	As above but for 6 children with a lower staff ratio.
TOTAL	**295,000**	

The advantages and dis-advantages of this type of budgeting technique can be summarised as follows:

Advantages
- Resources clearly matched to service provision
- Forms a base for unit costing
- Highlights which are the most expensive activities

Dis-Advantages
- Resource allocation may not be accurate
- Can be complex to calculate as detailed work needs to be undertaken to isolate each activity and the resources consumed
- Not practical for services where a flexible approach needs to be taken and where resources need to be moved between activities in response to demand

Contingency Budgeting

This budgeting technique is sometimes seen as "a broad brush" approach. Limited effort is used to establish detailed estimates for each of the budget headings as a contingency amount is provided within the budget to take account of poor estimates, changes in demand, and insufficient resources. The contingency may be used flexibly across any of the budget headings. The level of the contingency will depend on an estimation of the risk of error within the budget. If it is considered that the budget has been calculated to an accuracy level of 80%, then a 20% contingency may be added to the budget.

An example of the contingency approach is given as follows:

It is September and a nursery school is to develop a budget for next year. It's financial year runs from 1 April to 31 March.

Budget Heading	Budget Figures	Contingency Calculations
Salaries	200,000	Salaries for approximately 10 staff and some agency time if needed.
Food	40,000	Approximate food expenditure last year.
Supplies and Services	40,000	Approximate expected expenditure
Contingency	<u>20,000</u>	Will be used to supplement overspent budgets.
TOTAL	**300,000**	

The advantages and dis-advantages of this type of budgeting technique can be summarised as follows:

Advantages
- Quick
- Easy
- Flexible

Dis-Advantages
- Inaccurate; open to guess work
- Insufficient thought given to linking service with finance
- Will be difficult to monitor

Application of Budget Setting Techniques

Having considered a number of different budget setting techniques, it is clear that a combination of all these techniques may be utilised in creating a budget. For example:

Salary Budget

Incremental budgeting may be suitable if there is no change in establishment or if there is a resource restriction which states that staffing should remain constant.

Accommodation Budget

Rent and rates are usually fixed in nature and therefore could be subject to a cash limited or resource restricted budget.

Supplies and Services

These usually vary from year to year dependent upon what the organisation is trying to achieve. Quite often some of the budgets in this category are demand led and therefore difficult to predict. This will require a zero based approach with the addition of a contingency budget if the budget area is extremely volatile.

Income

Usually income will consist of fees and charges often related to specific activities. In this case an activity based approach to setting the budget may be the most appropriate.

Profiling Budgets

In addition to setting an annual budget it is also important to profile the budget. Profiling involves estimating how income and expenditure will arise over the year; for example, taking into account seasonal variations. The budget profile is fundamental to effective budget monitoring which will be discussed in the next chapter. For example, a budget profile for salaries should reflect the increments, pay awards and the known leavers and joiners during the year. A salary profile can be shown graphically as follows:

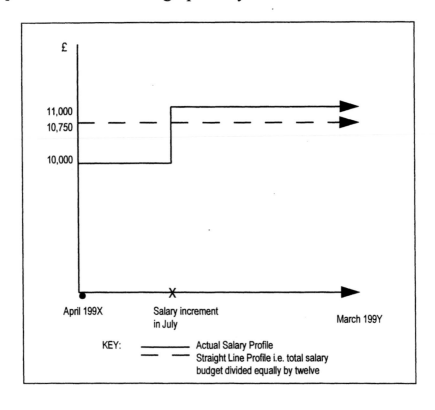

Diagram 3

Salaries increase from £10,000 per month to £11,000 per month as from July 199X onwards giving a total salary budget of £129,000. This is represented in diagram 3 by the solid line.

However, it is common practice to profile expenditure budgets equally across the twelve months of the year; this is referred to as a straight line profile. The dashed line in diagram 3 represents a straight line profile for the same £129,000 salary budget resulting in a monthly salary budget of £10,750. If the straight line approach is taken, it is quite evident that for each month the actual spend will differ from the straight line budget thus creating a variance each month. To aide the budget monitoring process, it is important to eliminate where at all possible differences which are due purely to profiling.

Common Budget Setting Practices

There are a number of budget setting practices which are commonly adopted by many public sector organisations. Some of these practices are highlighted below.

Vacancy factor/discount

It is quite common to calculate the total salary budget and then to reduce the budget by a vacancy factor. The logic behind this budgeting technique is that during the year there will always be a turnover of staff and hence there will always be a percentage of posts vacant. However, in a climate of high unemployment, many employees tend to stay in their posts for far longer and therefore the level of staff turnover is reduced. In these circumstances the scope for making savings through a vacancy factor is clearly more restricted.

Mid-point Salary Scales

In an organisation that uses scale rate salaries for graded posts, a common budgeting technique for salaries is to use the mid point of the salary scale. The logic is that this represents a good approximation of the average for all staff and therefore is an acceptable way of calculating an estimate. However, if most staff are at the top of their salary scale, this technique can result in a large under estimate of the salary budget.

Base Budgets

A base budget is sometimes called an original budget. Each year changes from the base budget are made usually using an incremental technique and adjustments made for any major changes. In the following year the adjustments are usually eliminated in order to return to the original base budget. This is an historic approach to budget setting and in some instances the assumptions behind the base budget may have been lost or forgotten and can be very far re-moved from the current service requirements.

Guess Work

Budgets for many items are often estimated using an educated guess. Ideally budgets should be based on written quotations, contract values, payroll information, etc. There should be very few areas that need to rely solely on guess work.

Arbitrary apportionment

Most budget estimates will have an element of this insofar as there will be central costs that need to be shared across different services. Even though there will be a need for apportionment, it should, where possible, be based on service use and not arbitrary methods such as number of employees, floor area, budget size, and so on.

SUMMARY

❏ A budget is a financial plan

❏ Budgets should ideally be linked to the business plan and be based on the organisation's objectives for the coming year

❏ Many organisations have a budget setting cycle identifying when the stages of the budget setting process takes place

❏ Budget setting may be top down; bottom up; or a combination of the two depending on the level of devolvement within an organisation

❏ A number of different budgeting techniques can be used when setting a budget. These include, incremental; zero based; cash limited; resource restricted; activity based; and contingency budgeting. It is quite possible to use elements of all these techniques when preparing a budget

❏ Budgets need to be profiled in order to assist with effective budgetary control

❏ Guess work should be kept to a minimum!

Exercise 3

Developing a Budget from First Principles

Take one of the following areas:

- ~   A Leisure Centre
- ~   A Secondary School
- ~   A Meals on Wheels Service
- ~   A Residential Nursing Home
- ~   A Contracts Management Unit
- ~   An Advice Centre
- ~   A Personnel Department
- ~   A Quality Assurance Division
- ~   A Hospital
- ~   A Fire Brigade

a)   For the area selected what are the first steps that you would take to prepare a zero based budget?

List Action Points Below:

b) In order to construct the budget, what would be the key income/expenditure items for the activity and how would you obtain the information in order to budget for them accurately?

List Key Income/Expenditure Areas   What Information would you
                                         need and where from?

c) Taking the complete list of services shown on the previous page, rank the activities in terms of their ease of budget setting in the order of 1 to 10, where 1 is the easiest.

Suggested solutions to this exercise can be found on page 138

Exercise 4

Incremental Budgeting

You are a budget manager and are responsible for input to the budget preparation.

You are required to produce some budget working papers as part of the preparation for the coming year's budget. The assumptions you have made in order to prepare the budget working papers are set out as follows.

ASSUMPTIONS FOR BUDGET PREPARATION

Your team consists of the following staff members:

Yourself, J Brown	(Basic Salary £40,000)
A Taylor	(Basic Salary £30,000)
P Pritkash	(Basic Salary £22,000)
C Doyle	(Basic Salary £20,000)
O Obayo	(Basic Salary £18,000)
D Lincoln	(Basic Salary £15,000)
R Cohen	(Basic Salary £13,200)

The negotiated pay awards for next year have been agreed as a percentage of basic salary with effect from 1 July. The percentages are as follows:

Salary Band	£35,000 and above	2.0%
Salary Band	£20,000 to £35,000	2.5%
Salary Band	Under £20,000	1.5%

National Insurance is calculated at 10.45%
Pension contributions are 6%

Other budgets will be based on last years figures which are summarised as follows:

Transport Costs	£10,000
Premises Costs	£50,000
Supplies and Services	£80,000
Financing Costs	£10,000

The inflation rate used for the transport, premises and supplies and services budget is 3%. Finance costs are to be inflated by 1%.

Assume the financial year runs from 1 April to 31 March

There is a new development you wish to implement this year to enhance the level of customer care. The development will require an on-line computer system and training for staff in telephone skills. The total cost should be calculated as follows:

- Five upgrades to existing terminals @ £1000 each

- A systems support hotline @ £2000 for the year additional administration of service £3000 per year

- Systems training for 5 staff @ £500 each

- Telephone skills training for 5 staff @ £200 each

A proforma budget working paper is set out on page 55 for calculation purposes.

Suggested solutions to this exercise can be found on page 140.

BUDGET WORKING PAPERS						
EMPLOYEE COSTS						
NAME	BASIC SALARY	PAY AWARD	TOTAL	N.I.	PENSION	BUDGET
TOTAL						

OPERATIONAL COSTS			
	COSTS LAST YEAR	INFLATION	BUDGET
TRANSPORT COSTS			
PREMISES COSTS			
SUPPLIES AND SERVICES			
NEW DEVELOPMENTS			
FINANCING COSTS			
TOTAL			
TOTAL BUDGET			

Exercise 5

Profiling Budgets

Using the spreadsheet on pages 58 and 59, profile the following budget heads and set out the projected monthly income and expenditure position (assume the financial year is 1 April to 31 March).

Salaries:
Based on current total staffing costs of £480,000 (inclusive). A pay award of 2% is due with effect from 1 July. One member of staff currently earning £36,000 (inclusive) is due to retire at the end of August and will not be replaced.

Central Recharges:
These will be based on Service Level Agreements for central services and will be charged quarterly. The total amount for the year has been estimated at £80,000.

Supplies and Services:
The total budget for these services is £60,000, however, there is no historic information on how expenditure arises for these items.

Transport Costs:
It is usual that only 25% of the total budget is spent in the first half of the year and 75% in the second half of the year. The total budget for transport is £18,000.

Professional Fees:

These arise on an adhoc basis as and when they are needed. It is difficult to predict the level of expenditure each year as it fluctuates tremendously based on the case loads. A total budget of £120,000 has been set, with a view that the contingency budget may have to be used.

Contingency:

A contingency has been established as part of the budget this year. This is in order to provide for incorrect estimates, unforeseen events, and fluctuating demand. The total contingency allowed for the year has been set at 10% of all expenditure heads.

Fees:

Having examined historic records and spoken to internal customers, an estimate for fees has been established at approximately £900,000. It has been assumed that fees will arise equally over the year as a basis for profiling.

Suggested solutions to this exercise can be found on page 142.

PROFILED BUDGET

	April	May	June	July	August	Sept.
Income						
Fees						
Total						
Expenditure						
Salaries						
Central Recharges						
Supplies and Services						
Transport Costs						
Professional Fees						
Contingency						
Total						
Surplus/Deficit Month						

Oct.	Nov	Dec.	Jan.	Feb.	March	TOTAL

Exercise 6

Budget Setting in your Organisation

a)   Describe the current budget setting process and your involvement with the process.

b)   Who is responsible for agreeing the final budget and when are you made aware of your budget?

c)   How could the budget setting process be improved?   This includes from initial stages through to the issue of the final budget.

Chapter 4

BUDGETARY CONTROL

Budgetary control is about managing the monies allocated to a particular budget, as well as ensuring that funds are properly utilised with respect to the level and quality of output required from those financial resources.

For example:

If questioned, many budget holders would say they are capable of managing a furniture budget of £10,000, meaning that they would ensure that the £10,000 furniture budget was not over spent. However, this is only one aspect of budget management. In order to fully manage the budget, the budget holder needs to know what the £10,000 budget was expected to purchase (quantity and quality) and over what time frame.

If the objectives for a £10,000 furniture budget is to purchase 100 typist chairs without arms, of average quality over the next three months, the budget holder may then begin to manage the budget. The budget holder will not just monitor the amount of money being spent on the chairs during the period but also the number of chairs being purchased with the budget, and the quality of those chairs.

> *The budget holder may consider that they have performed well if they are able to purchase the correct number and quality of chairs for less than £10,000. Therefore, in order to adequately manage a budget, the budget holder has to know both the quantity of service/product to be provided and the quality standard that needs to be met. Budgetary control will then involve monitoring the money, the quantity and quality of the output.*

Monitoring and Managing the Budget

To ensure effective budgetary control, budgets have to be monitored and managed. In some organisations these functions are separated. If the budgets are delegated, then the budget holder may only undertake monitoring with no real power to manage the budget. If the budget is fully devolved, then the budget holder will both monitor and manage the budget. The difference between monitoring and managing budgets is not clearly defined, however, they can be broadly distinguished as follows:

Monitoring Budgets ⇨ Checking accuracy of actual income and expenditure; comparing actuals with budgets; comparing actual with expected outputs; identifying trends; highlighting areas of over and under spending to the person managing the budget.

Managing Budgets ⇨ As a result of detailed monitoring, taking the necessary action to ensure the budget remains in control.

Just how much ability a budget holder has to both monitor and manage will depend on the decision making structure within the organisation.

Budgetary Control Process

The process of controlling budgets can be broken down into a number of stages:

Establish Actual Position

For this there will be a need to examine the financial management information that is available within the organisation. (The range of financial information that should be available is discussed in chapter 5). Depending on the quality of reports produced by the organisation, there may be a need for other records to be maintained, sometimes by the budget holder, or front-line staff. The actual position will have to take account of committed expenditure. (See commitment accounting later in this chapter).

Compare Actual with Budget

The difference between the actual and budgeted figures results in a variance. Variance analysis is an important tool in the budgetary control process. Variance analysis is discussed in detail in the next section.

Establish reasons for Variances

There are a number of reasons why the actual and budgeted figures differ. The reasons for any variance needs to be identified. This process is critical to gaining effective control as the budget holder needs to know when it is appropriate to take corrective action.

Take Action

Budgets are only being managed if action is taken to control them. There are a number of actions that a budget holder may take to establish effective control. These are set out later in this chapter.

Variance Analysis

In the context of budgetary control, the term variance refers to the difference between actual and budget. An example of a variance is shown as follows:

Month 6			
Budget Heading	Budget to Date	Actual to Date	Variance
Salaries	£120,000	£132,000	(£12,000)

The above example shows that by the six month period, the budgeted expenditure on salaries was £120,000, however, actual spending on salaries for those six months totalled £132,000. The difference between these two figures is £12,000 which represents the variance from the budget. In this case the variance is negative, hence the brackets, representing an overspend.

Budget to date will show the amount of the budget that should have been spent by month 6. Ideally the budget will be profiled to reflect the pattern of spending over the year such that when the actual expenditure during the period is compared with the budget, the true variance is calculated.

A more comprehensive variance statement is shown below.

Month 6								
Budget Heading	Budget for the Month	Actual for the Month	Variance	%	Budget to Date	Actual to Date	Variance	%
Salaries	50,000	53,000	(3,000)	6	120,000	132,000	(12,000)	10

This statement shows the variance for the month as well as the year to date. The variance for the month is often referred to as the **discrete** as opposed to the year to date which is referred to as the **cumulative**.

Variances can be expressed in terms of figures or percentages. Clearly, a budget holder needs to know the amount of over or underspend, however, it is also useful to know what proportion of the budget has been over or under-spent. The over or underspend could be a large amount but only represent a small proportion of the total budget. The action taken as a result of a variance will depend on both its amount and proportion in relation to the budget.

Establishing Actuals

In order to establish a true variance, it is important that the actual expenditure recorded is accurate. Actual expenditure at any particular point in time will include the following elements:

❖ Goods and Services that have been paid for

❖ Goods and Services that have been used as at that date but not paid for, these items may be represented by invoices unpaid (creditors) or by accruals (estimates of amounts used during the period even though invoices have not yet been received, e.g. telephone bills)

All actual expenditure should be charged to the budget heading to which it relates. If the budget has been correctly constructed, there should be little difficulty in identifying where the actual expenditure should be charged. It is usual for an accounting system to be used whereby codes are allocated to each budget heading. Many organisations operate computerised accounting systems which allocate the actual expenditure to the code or codes given. Ideally, the budget holder should be responsible for the coding, even if it is undertaken by someone else. At the very minimum, the budget holder should be aware of the codes that have been allocated to each of the budget headings under his/her control and should ensure that actual expenditure is always coded correctly.

Commitment Accounting

In order to have a full awareness of their true position, a budget holder should to know not only the actual expenditure at any point in time but also what expenditure has been committed at that point. Committed expenditure relates to elements of the budget that have been formerly allocated to future expenditure such as orders or contracts. By calculating the committed expenditure, the budget holder is able to identify the true balance remaining of a budget and to establish variances against planned expenditure and commitments. Commitment accounting will provide the budget holder with a tighter control of the budget and will throw greater light on the reasons for variances as commitments tend to reflect future activities.

In order to operate a commitment accounting system, it is important to have a method of identifying goods and services that have been committed to. This is usually achieved by way of an order, contract, etc. which commits the organisation to purchase goods or use services.

Reasons for Variances

There are a number of reasons why variances occur, the most common of which are identified as follows:

Mis-coding » Wrong account code used

Error » Incorrect figures entered onto the accounting system

Delays » Delays in entering information onto the accounting system

Profiling » Often incorrect budget profiles are entered which bear no relevance to the pattern of actual expenditure (e.g. no account taken of seasonal fluctuations)

Poor Budgeting » Little consideration given to initial budget preparation

Unplanned Changes » Such as increases and decreases in demand for services, or introduction of new legislation

Poor Management » Where a budget has been properly prepared but badly managed. For example, lights are left on 24 hours a day causing waste and hence overspending of the electric budget. Conversely, good management may lead to savings on the budget

Projecting the Outturn

In order to fully control the budget, it is important to keep focusing on the future position. The calculation of the **outturn** becomes an important process as it reflects the projected financial position at the end of the year. The projected outturn should be calculated on a regular basis taking into account assumptions about changes to the budgeted expenditure during the year.

An illustration of how the projected outturn may be calculated is shown as follows:

Financial Management Report - Month 6					
Account Description	Total Budget	Budget to Date	Actual to Date	Projected Outturn	Projected (over)/ underspend for year
Salaries	250,000	125,000	135,000	270,000	(20,000)

The projected outturn of £270,000 in the above example assumes that spending continues into the second six months at the same rate as in the previous six months. This projection is based on an even arithmetic progression over the 12 months and a general formula for this type of calculation is given as follows:

$$\frac{\text{Amount Spent to Date}}{\text{Number of months to date}} \quad \text{x} \quad 12 \quad = \quad \text{Projected Outturn}$$

If a budget has extremely variable expenditure each month, or where there are known changes to occur in the future with respect to the budget, both these aspects need to be taken into account when calculating the projected outturn. Using the above example, if it is known that a member of staff is leaving the organisation, the projected outturn should be adjusted downwards to reflect the salary reduction. If there are no adjustments, the projected outturn should continue to reflect the original expenditure profile of the budget.

Virement

This is a common word used in the public sector and refers to a particular process which can be used in the following ways:

❖ the establishment of new budgets

❖ the amendment of an existing budget

The process involves moving funds from one budget heading to another budget heading and so is only possible if there is a budget to vire from. For example, if there is a clothing budget of £3,000 and no budget for equipment, it would be possible to vire an amount from the clothing budget, say £1,500, and establish an equipment budget. Virements are used for corrective action whereby a budget that has been underspent can be used to increase a budget that has been overspent. The effect of this is to change the budgeted amounts for each area to more accurately reflect the current spending position.

Taking Corrective Action

There are a number of actions that can be taken by a budget holder when attempting to control an over or underspent budget. These include:

For Budget Overspend	**For Budget Underspend**
❖ Reduce or halt expenditure	❖ Increase income
❖ Increase income	❖ Decrease income
❖ Make virements	❖ Make virements
❖ Use contingency funds	❖ Save contingency funds
❖ Delay activities	❖ Bring forward activities
❖ Re-define objective	❖ Re-define objectives
❖ Re-define eligibility criteria	❖ Re-define eligibility criteria
❖ Change nature of the service	❖ Change the nature of the service
❖ Cease or reduce service delivery	❖ Increase service delivery

Controllable and Uncontrollable Budgets

The following diagram illustrates the process for identifying an uncontrollable budget.

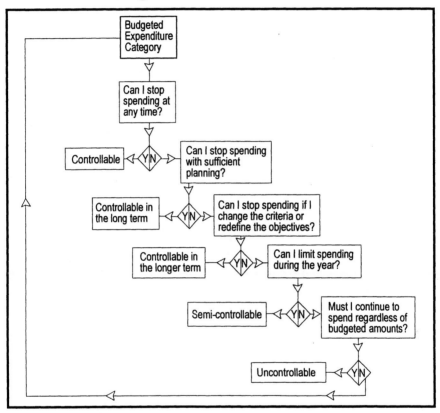

Diagram 4

It is relatively easy to identify actions that may be taken with respect to controllable budgets. However, if overspending occurs with an uncontrollable budget it may be necessary to take action with regards to controllable budgets in order to identify additional funds to meet the uncontrollable overspend. This is often the case when there is a demand led statutory service which cannot be halted regardless of the level of spending. Funding for this will often be at the expense of reductions in expenditure on non statutory activities.

Controlling Income Budgets

Income budgets should be based on a detailed income forecast which clearly identifies where each of the sources of income are to be found. Income budgets which rely heavily on user contributions, such as leisure centre entrance fees, are generally more difficult to control. In such cases the income budget is fundamental to overall budgetary control and requires considerable management. In order to adequately control income, the following issues are important:

❖ Ensure that a detailed monthly projection has been produced that is correctly profiled based on past experience and future expectation

❖ Regular projected outturns should be calculated

❖ Where applicable, the marketing plan needs to be closely allied to the expected income targets as a result of marketing activities. Marketing plans need to be changed if income targets are not being met

❖ Original income estimates should always be prudently developed due to the unpredictable nature of certain types of income

❖   If income is to be a fixed amount under contract, the contract terms need to be monitored

❖   If there is a trend of under-achievement on income, the corrective action steps should be taken as previously listed

SUMMARY

- ☐ Budgetary control is not only about controlling the money, it is also about controlling the output resulting from the financial resource input

- ☐ Effective budgetary control involves both monitoring and managing the budget

- ☐ The budgetary control process compares actual spending with budgeted spending and takes action to correct variations

- ☐ Commitment accounting takes into account expenditure that has been committed such as orders for goods and services

- ☐ Projecting the outturn is a useful budgetary control technique which should be regularly undertaken so as to provide an up to date assessment of the year end position

- ☐ Corrective action should be taken if actual spending is very different from the budget. This would include actions such as virements

- ☐ Income budgets require as much control as expenditure budgets

Exercise 7

Variance Analysis

1. Give your interpretation of the following variances; examine each line independently.

Month 6 Report (September)

		ACTUAL	BUDGET	VARIANCE	ACTUAL YTD	BUDGET YTD	VARIANCE
a)	Salaries	2200	2000	(200)	12200	12000	(200)
b)	Salaries	2000	2000	(0)	12000	12000	(0)
c)	Salaries	2200	2000	(200)	13200	12000	(1200)
d)	Salaries	1200	2000	800	12200	12000	(200)
e)	Salaries	2400	2000	(400)	12200	12000	(200)
f)	Salaries	2000	2000	(0)	12400	12000	(400)
g)	Salaries	1800	2000	200	11800	12000	200

2. Give four examples of what may cause a variance in your area of work.

3. Give two examples of uncontrollable variances in your area of work.

4. As a budget holder, what key control mechanisms could you apply to bring variances under control.

Suggested solutions to this exercise can be found on page 144.

Exercise 8

The Role of the Budget Holder

You have been given the responsibility for a furniture budget for the entire office which includes four separate floors with each floor housing a separate division. The budget has been cash limited at £40,000 for the year. This figure has been developed by the accountant who took last years budget and applied zero growth. As budget holder you are responsible for approving all expenditure on furniture and requests have to be made to you by the divisional heads.

In the past there has been wide disgruntlement for several reasons

- *There appeared to be no control of the budget as it was always spent by month 6, and anyone who had not ordered furniture in the first half of the year had to go without*

- *Some divisions had substantially more spent on them than others regardless of their relative size*

- *There appeared to be no choice in the type of furniture received, e.g. chairs always came in the same colour regardless of the one ordered due to "bulk" purchasing*

- *The budget was not previously devolved to a particular person and was administered by finance on a first come first served basis with no assessment of need*

- *Some divisions think that suppliers were paid for furniture that was never actually received as deliveries are usually made directly to the floor in question and invoices sent separately to the finance department who never appeared to check*

As the new budget holder you are determined to ensure that such complaints cease and that the budget is properly managed. There have been rumours that performance related pay increments will be related to how well budgets are managed and so you have a personal interest in the whole process.

Questions:

a)   What steps do you think need to be taken from the beginning of the year in order to ensure that the budget is well controlled?

b)   What systems need to be in place to assist the budget holder to maintain control during the year?

c)   How will the budget holder manage to stop the complaints this year?

Suggested solutions to this exercise can be found on page 146.

Exercise 9

Budgetary Control in Your Organisation

1) Describe the current process of budgetary control in your organisation?

2) How are you involved in the control process?

3) Do you consider budgets are adequately controlled in all areas within your organisation, and if not, how do you think budgetary control can be improved?

Chapter 5

FINANCIAL MANAGEMENT INFORMATION

A financial management information system (FMIS) is used to record and process transactions of a financial nature and then to provide financial information.

Financial information arising from FMIS's are used for a variety of purposes but most typically, they are used as the basis for preparing the annual audited financial accounts as well as providing management accounting information. The difference between the audited financial accounts and the internally focused management accounts are highlighted as follows:

FINANCIAL ACCOUNTS	MANAGEMENT ACCOUNTS
❖ Standard financial statements which have to be prepared in a recognised format	❖ Tailor made statements and reports which can be presented in any format as desired by the user
❖ External orientation, as they will be available in the public domain	❖ Internal orientation, as they should only be seen by the user of the information
❖ Required by law to be prepared on a regular basis - annually	❖ Prepared as often as deemed useful - could be daily reports
❖ Reports on the past. Accounts are made up on a historic basis reporting transactions and activities that have already taken place	❖ Looks to the future. Management accounts contain budgetary information for the year ahead and considers how past activities will impact on that budget in the future
❖ Tends to cover a broad area of activity	❖ Tends to cover a specific area of activity
❖ Reports have to conform to external standards	❖ Reports only conform to internal standards within the organisation if they exist

Of the above, it is typically the management accounting information that a budget holder will require on an ongoing basis to control his/her budget.

Management Accounts

Ideally the management accounts that are produced by the FMIS should display the following characteristics (AEIOU).

Accurate
Easy to understand
Informative
On time
Up-to-date

Each of these attributes are discussed further on the following pages:

Accurate

It is important that financial management information is accurate and can be relied upon otherwise its integrity will fall into disrepute and may be disregarded by the users. Accuracy is achieved by ensuring that the information entering the FMIS is correctly processed. For example, the payment of an invoice will only be accurately entered onto the FMIS if:

❖ the arithmetic is checked

❖ the description of the goods or service has been checked as correct and received

❖ the allocation of the payment is correct and goes against the appropriate budget

❖ the payment is authorised

Easy to understand

Management accounts are often prepared for budget holders who have little or no formal financial training. Management accounts therefore need to be set out in a simple fashion that can be followed easily by a budget holder who may have limited financial awareness.

Informative

In addition to being very clear, the information contained in the accounts needs to be relevant to the budget holder and provide the budget holder with the information that he/she thinks they need in order to control their budgets. The type and format of information contained in the management accounts will vary depending on the type of service and the budget holders own preferences. For example, some budget holders prefer their variances stated as percentages as opposed to being shown as a positive or negative figure. Variances are discussed in detail in chapter 4.

On time

Budget holders do require regular information in order to enable them to exercise adequate control. It is normal for management accounts to be produced on a regular basis, often monthly, but management accounts may be required more frequently for some budgets. It is important for the providers of the information to work to a timetable so that budget holders can rely on information being available when they need it. In some organisations there is sufficient flexibility for reports to be produced on demand, otherwise it is normal for a monthly report to be produced a specified number of days after the month end.

Up to date

Budget holders need to be aware of the currency of the management accounting information. So if, for example, the management accounting report is dated September, the budget holder needs to know that transactions have been processed up until say, the end of August. In some cases information may lag even further behind due to the systems operated by the organisation and the speed of data processing.

Styles of Reporting

Management accounts may be presented in a range of styles to meet the needs of the budget holder. An example of a report for a residential home is shown on the following page.

Budgetary Control Report

Cost Centre No: 635
Centre Desc: Lodge House

Report for Month: 12
Month End: 28/03/X3

1 19X1/X2 Actuals	2 Account No	3 Account Description	4 19X2/X3 Estimate	5 Payments/Income Current Mth	6 Estimate to Date	7 Payments/ Income to Date	8 Var %	9 Outstanding Commits	10 Total Incl. Commits	11 Spend %
		Employee Exp.								
112,500	A100	Salaries - Admin	98,500	9,300	98,500	110,400	12	0	110,400	112
64,000	B300	Wages - Domestic	42,000	4,720	42,000	56,640	35	0	56,640	135
12,500	B310	Temporary Staff	0	900	0	9,800	0	400	10,200	0
1,500	C400	Subsistence	500	100	500	1,400	180	200	1,600	320
190,500		*Total Employee Exp.	141,000	15,020	141,000	178,240	26	600	178,840	127
		Premises Exp.								
4,000	D510	Rents & Rates	4,000	0	4,000	0	-100	3,000	3,000	75
2,500	D806	Utilities	3,000	0	3,000	3,600	20	0	3,600	120
750	D940	Cleaning	750	100	750	800	7	0	800	107
250	D967	Sundry	150	100	500	1,000	100	0	1,000	667
7,500		*Total Premises Exp.	7,900	200	8,250	5,400	-35	3,000	8,400	106
		Supplies and Services								
4,000	F005	Equipment	6,000	2,000	6,000	2,500	-58	3,000	5,500	92
1,200	F300	Printing & Stationery	600	100	600	750	25	0	750	125
13,000	F510	Provisions	12,500	1,200	12,500	14,000	12	0	14,000	112
1,000	F530	Clothing	1,000	0	1,000	100	-90	0	100	10
19,200		* Total Supplies & Services	20,100	3,300	20,100	17,350	-14	3,000	20,350	101
217,200		** Total Expenditure	169,000	18,520	169,350	200,990	19	6,600	207,590	123
		Income								
167,000	R700	Fees & Charges	169,000	12,000	169,000	154,000	-9	0	154,000	91
167,000		* Total Income	169,000	12,000	169,000	154,000	-9	0	154,000	91
50,200		*** Net Expenditure	0	6,520	350	46,990		6,600	53,590	

The report shows a number of columns which are explained as follows:

Column No.   Column Heading

1   **Actuals for the previous years**
States the actual figures for the previous year by cost centre code.

Column No.   Column Heading

2   Account Number
Provides a unique code for each expenditure and income account heading. Some codes will be unique to the cost centre whilst other codes are the same for all cost centres. This allows for aggregation and consolidation of budgetary information for a number of different cost centres in order to present financial information for a whole service.

3   Account Description
This gives an abbreviated description of the account, and the type of expenditure which should relate to the account code.

4   Estimate
This gives the budget for the current financial year. This terminology is used by local authorities, however, other terms used to describe this column include:

> - *annual budget, and*
> - *forecast year*

5   Payments/Income Current Month
This column shows the total of all transactions for the current month against the relevant account codes. In this example the column identifies transactions in month 12. If the budget holder requires to gain a further understanding of the figures presented on the report, a further report may be produced, usually called a transactions analysis. The transaction analysis identifies the individual transactions behind each figure.

Column No.   Column Heading

6   **Estimate to Date**
               This identifies how much of the budget should have
               been spent/received to date. Ideally this column
               should be profiled according to planned expenditure
               and in some organisations is referred to as the
               profiled budget.

7   **Payments/Income to Date**
               This shows the actual cumulative figure for the
               period. As the report is for month 12, this column
               shows 12 months of expenditure and income.

8   **Variance Percentage**
               This produces a calculation which takes column 6
               from column 7 and divides the result by column 6.
               The variance shows how much of the budget is
               under/over spent as a percentage, or in the case of
               income, the over/under achievement percentage.
               Therefore, in the case of total employee expenses,
               there is a 26% overspend.

9   **Outstanding Commitments**
               One of the purposes of this column is to identify
               items that have been ordered but not yet paid for.
               When the budget holder orders goods, an amount
               equal to the order can be established as a
               commitment. The commitment is then cancelled
               when the invoice is received and paid. The use of
               this column helps the budget holder to obtain a
               better understanding of what is available to spend.

Column No.   Column Heading

10   Total including Commitments
This takes the total payments to date column and adds it to the commitments. It is this total that is then used in column 11 to show the percentage of budget that has been spent and committed to date.

11   Percentage Spend
This takes column 11 as a percentage of column 4, i.e. the total spend plus commitments divided by the total budget. Given this is a month 12 report it would be acceptable to expect that each heading was 100% spent. However, it can be seen that some items are in excess of, or below 100%.

It should be noted that this report does raise some interesting anomalies:

❖   Expenditure is coded to accounts where no budget has been allocated, for example, temporary staff; *This could occur due to poor planning, e.g. when a budget head which should have been created has been forgotten, or if an error has arisen as a result of a mis-coding*

❖   Budgets exist for which no actual spend has occurred, for example rents and rates; *Again, this could be due to poor planning when budget heads which are now redundant have not been deleted or due to mis-coding of legitimate budget spend elsewhere*

Using the Financial Management Information

Budgetary control reports should provide the budget holder with useful financial management information that can be utilised for decision making. In particular, such reports should highlight key points such as:

❖ Which accounts are under or overspent

❖ How much of the budget has been spent so far

❖ Whether current expenditure is in line with planned expenditure - i.e. the budget profiles

❖ How does current expenditure compare with last years actual expenditure

❖ The potential to make virements from one expenditure budget to another

(The same points are relevant for income budgets)

The extent to which the reported information can be relied upon depends largely on the quality of information entered onto the FMIS. For example budget profiles may be incorrect; items may have been incorrectly coded; or the information may be very out of date. Ideally, budget holders should have easy access to the FMIS, and in the case of a computerised system, budget holders should ideally have the ability to interrogate information on screen.

Management accounts will be produced in a wide variety of formats depending largely on individual user requirements. However, in all cases, the budget holder will require the following basic information:

Account information	⇨	including account title, description, code, etc.
Budget information	⇨	including total budgets, period budgets (monthly/quarterly), and profiled budgets
Variance analysis	⇨	showing the difference between actual and planned expenditure/income, either in total monetary terms, or as a percentage, or both

Ideally budget holders should provide input into the report format in order to ensure the desired information requirements are achieved from the report. Many budget holders require the production of additional information such as statistics and details of activity in order to further assist in the interpretation of performance. Examples of additional information produced for budget holders include:

❖ Percentage of budget spent to date compared with previous year

❖ Percentage of over and under spend on each budget

❖ Average spend per day or per month

❖ Average spend per client/per transaction/per employee/or any relevant activity, e.g. for a fire service the budget holder may wish to know average spend per call out, or average spend per fire, etc.

❖ Trends of spend each month showing percentage increases/decreases month on month

If the budget holder is also responsible for generating income and has income targets, then similar statistics should be developed for income along with ratios linking income to expenditure, e.g. the margin of surplus or deficit on the activity.

SUMMARY

❏ Financial management information systems are used to record transactions of a financial nature and to provide financial information

❏ Financial management information acts as a basis for the production of annual audited accounts as well as management accounts

❏ Financial management information should ideally have the AEIOU characteristics

❏ Financial reports can be presented in a variety of styles. The benefit of management accounting is that the financial information is designed to meet the needs of the budget holder

❏ Budget holders should ideally input into the design of the report format. In addition, budget holders may require information such as statistics and details of activity in order to fully interpret performance

Exercise 10

Understanding Financial Management Information

You have been given the management accounts of a school for children with special needs to review (shown on page 92).

a)   *What is your initial reaction to the range of variances and what immediate additional information do you require in order to assist in your decision making about the variances?*

b)   *Given that it is month 6 (half way through the financial year), what actions do you expect to be taken in the short term, and what actions would you expect to take in the long term?*

c)   *What management techniques should be used when attempting to get the suggested actions implemented by other staff?*

d)   *What other monitoring processes would you adopt in order to satisfactorily take control of the situation?*

e)   *Calculate the projected outturn for the year, based on the assumptions given on page 94 (use the proforma on page 95).*

XYZ School
Management Accounts

	Month 6 Actual £	Month 6 Budgeted £	Variance £		Explanatory Notes	YTD Actual £	YTD Budgeted £	Variance £	
INCOME									
Fees	8,000	14,000	6,000	U		54,000	84,000	30,000	U
Revenue Grant	10,000	3,333	6,667	F		20,000	20,000	-	
Special Grant	30,000	15,000	15,000	F	1	30,000	30,000	-	
Donations	100	240	140	U		500	1,200	700	U
Other	-	2,000	2,000	U		1,000	12,000	11,000	U
	48,100	34,573				105,500	147,200		
EXPENDITURE									
Salaries	10,000	12,000	2,000	F	2	66,000	72,000	6,000	F
Temp Salaries	3,000	500	2,500	U	2	7,000	3,000	4,000	U
Rent	1,500	500	1,000	U		3,000	3,000	-	
Gas	1,000	300	700	U		1,600	1,800	200	F
Electricity	1,200	400	800	U		2,400	2,400	-	
Telephone	900	200	700	U		2,100	1,200	900	U
Food	5,000	3,000	2,000	U		28,000	18,000	10,000	U
Equipment Hire	800	500	300	U		4,800	3,000	1,800	U
Maintenance	1,000	200	800	U		1,000	1,200	200	F
Cleaning	300	200	100	U		1,100	1,200	100	F
Travel and Subsistence	300	100	200	U		1,200	600	600	U
Staff Expenses	500	100	400	U		1,400	600	800	U
Laundry	200	200	-			1,400	1,200	200	U
Computer	-	5,000	5,000	F	3	-	10,000	10,000	F
Furniture and Equipment	8,000	5,000	3,000	U	3	10,000	10,000	-	
Major Repairs	7,000	5,000	2,000	U	3	11,000	10,000	1,000	U
Sundry	800	373	427	U		1,800	2,000	200	F
	41,500	33,573				143,800	141,200		
Recharges/Allocation of central costs	2,500	1,000	1,500	U		12,500	6,000	6,500	U
TOTAL	44,000	34,573				156,300	147,200		
Surplus/(Deficit)	4,100	-				(50,800)			

KEY

F =   Favourable

U =   Unfavourable

YTD =   Year to date

Explanatory Notes

1.   Special grant should have been released in two stages, quarter 1 and quarter 2, however, the quarter 1 grant was received late.

2.   There are two staff vacancies due to recruitment problems and agency staff have been used for cover.

3.   These are areas of expenditure for which the special grant has been given.

Suggested solutions to this exercise can be found on page 148.

PROJECTED OUTTURN ASSUMPTIONS

a) Spending on food will only be 50% of that in the first half of the year.

b) Staff expenses will no longer be authorised.

c) Computer will be purchased in the second half of the year but a £1,000 virement will be made from this heading to compensate for the over spend on major repairs.

d) All other headings have been assumed to continue at the same rate as in the first six months.

The projected outturn solution can be found on page 152.

Proforma Worksheet
To Calculate Projected Outturn

	Month 6 Actual £	Month 6 Budgeted £		Projected Outturn £
INCOME:				
Fees	54,000	84,000		
Revenue Grant	20,000	20,000		
Special Grant	30,000	30,000		
Donations	500	1,200		
Other	1,000	12,000		_____
	105,500	147,200		_____
EXPENDITURE:				
Salaries	66,000	72,000		
Temp. Salaries	7,000	3,000		
Rent	3,000	3,000		
Gas	1,600	1,800		
Electricity	2,400	2,400		
Telephone	2,100	1,200		
Food	28,000	18,000	(a)	
Equipment Hire	4,800	3,000		
Maintenance	1,000	1,200		
Cleaning	1,100	1,200		
Travel and Subsistence	1,200	600		
Staff Expenses	1,400	600	(b)	
Laundry	1,400	1,200		
Computer	-	10,000	(c)	
Furniture and Equipment	10,000	10,000		
Major Repairs	11,000	10,000		
Sundry	1,800	2,000		_____
	143,800	141,200		
Recharges	12,500	6,000		_____
	156,300	147,200		
Overspend	(50,800)			_____

Exercise 11

Establishing Your Financial Management Information Needs

Complete the following questionnaire

1) What size of budget(s) has been (or will be) devolved to you?

    a) up to £10,000

    b) £10,001 - £50,000

    c) £50,001 - £100,000

    d) £100,001 - £250,000

    e) over £250,000

2) How many transactions do you expect during the year?

    a) less than 4

    b) 5 to 10

    c) 11 to 25

    d) 26 to 100

    e) over 100

3)   How often do the transactions take place?

    a)   annually

    b)   half yearly

    c)   monthly

    d)   weekly

    e)   daily

4)   How simple is the budget(s) to control?

    a)   very simple

    b)   simple

    c)   moderate

    d)   quite difficult

    e)   very difficult

5)   What is the risk of overspending?

    a)   very low

    b)   low

    c)   moderate

    d)   high

    e)   very high

6) How easily can your main budget (the highest value) be profiled?

a)	very easily	
b)	moderately	
c)	with some difficulty	
d)	with great difficulty	
e)	cannot be profiled	

7) How would you describe the volatility of your main budget(s)?

a)	static	
b)	mildly fluctuating	
c)	moderately fluctuating	
d)	very volatile	
e)	totally unpredictable	

8) How do you rate the importance of the devolved budgets for which you are responsible, in relation to the total expenditure/performance of the organisation?

a)	not important	
b)	moderately important	
c)	important	
d)	very important	
e)	a critical budget	

9) How do you rate your competency as a financial manager?

    a)   very good

    b)   good

    c)   average

    d)   poor

    e)   very poor

10) How seriously are devolved budgets being taken in your organisation?

    a)   not seriously

    b)   quite seriously

    c)   seriously

    d)   very seriously

    e)   budgetary control linked to

         performance related pay

Suggested solutions to this exercise can be found on page 153.

Exercise 12

Financial Management Information

Take a copy of a typical financial management report produced by your organisation:

* Consider how it measures up to the characteristics of good financial information:

  Is it **A**ccurate?
  Is it **E**asy to understand?
  Is it **I**nformative?
  Is it **O**n time?
  Is it **U**p to date?

Chapter 6

MANAGEMENT AND FINANCIAL RESPONSIBILITY

Management Responsibility

In establishing a devolved budget, ideally financial and management responsibilities should be aligned. This means the person responsible for making management decisions about the service is also the person responsible for the budget. In the context of budgetary control, management responsibilities refer to those responsibilities that relate to the day to day aspects of service delivery. Therefore, a budget holder will have management responsibilities if:

❖ They have the ability to make decisions about resources used to deliver a service

❖ They have the ability to increase or decrease service levels (quantity and/or quality)

❖ They have the ability to influence the way in which the service is delivered (even if this is only controlling their own method of working)

The following example illustrates the previous points:

A cook will have the day to day responsibility for food preparation, menus, and perhaps supervision of other catering staff. The budgets devolved to the cook would be those of food purchasing and some aspects of the salary budget such as overtime or temporary staffing. The management responsibilities will involve the cook deciding whether or not to purchase in bulk or to buy on a daily basis; the types of suppliers that are used; the content of the menus; and hence the types of food purchases to be made. In some public sector organisations, the cook may be divorced from such management decisions, and there may be a central purchasing unit that takes responsibility for all purchases and selects the approved suppliers. If this is the case, then it would be unfair to devolve such budgets to the cook because the cook has no management responsibilities with respect to the service output, i.e. the meals prepared will be determined by the ingredients that have been made available to this budget holder.

The involvement of the budget holder in budget setting is very important to the management process as the budget holder needs to be totally clear as to the outputs that are expected from the allocated budget. Even if the budget holder has had no involvement in the development of the budgets, he/she should be briefed as to the output/results that the devolved budget is expected to produce. If this information is not forthcoming, the budget holder has to develop a clear idea as to what can realistically be achieved with the budget and then create his/her own targets. Therefore, our cook should be aware of the number of meals that need to be provided with the catering budget.

Financial Responsibility

A budget holder's financial responsibilities will include the following:

❖ Checking that payments are only made for goods and services that have been received

❖ Authorising invoices for payment

❖ Coding payments to the correct account

❖ Checking that the actual transactions on each budget heading is correct

❖ Arranging for errors to be corrected

❖ Monitoring actual expenditure/income against budgets

In order to meet their financial responsibilities, the budget holder should ideally have some involvement with the design format of the financial information being provided. This may mean liaising with an accountant or/an accounts department, or it may mean becoming familiar with the computerised financial systems where the budget holder has on-line access.

Most organisations operate some form of computerised accounting systems and depending on the organisation and the level of devolvement in place, budget holders may have different levels of access to the financial systems. Several different levels of access are described on the following page.

No Access	⇨	Budget holders do not have access to a terminal and only receive printed reports. Requests need to be made to the accounting department for other information.
General Access	⇨	Budget holder has access to a terminal and a more general "look-up" facility along with the ability to generate reports to be printed locally.
On line Access	⇨	Budget holder has a terminal and a facility whereby they may effect transactions such as making payments and entering commitments.

In order to adequately discharge the financial responsibilities of a budget holder, it is essential that there is a good working relationship with the providers of financial information such as the accounts departments.

Linking Management and Financial Responsibilities

A key to successful devolved budgetary responsibility is ensuring that financial and management responsibilities are aligned, as the two issues are linked. In introducing devolved budgetary responsibilities, some organisations have encountered very real problems by missing this essential point.

If the budget holder has management responsibility without financial responsibility, and wishes to make a management decision about the service which requires the use of the budget, then this may create problems. For example, the budget holder may have to go through a long process of obtaining authorisation, and in some cases, he/she may be told that the budget cannot be spent in a particular manner or that the budget has already been fully committed. This inhibits the way in which the service can be effectively delivered by slowing down the decision making process and creating inefficiencies generally.

If the budget holder has financial responsibility without management responsibility, budgetary control can again be very difficult. This is due to the fact that other people may make decisions about service delivery without the budget holder's knowledge. If overspending occurs, the budget holder will still be held accountable even though the cause was not a result of their decision.

Accountability

An important element of successful devolved budgetary control is having an effective process for accountability. The budget holder will have no incentive to undertake the financial responsibilities if there is no method of accountability. Effective accountability can be achieved in several different ways.

❖ Through the line manager system

❖ Through the performance appraisal system

❖   Through a service contract agreement

❖   Through the pay and benefits system

❖   Through the board/committee structures

Each of the above approaches are discussed below:

Line Manager

Formal or informal reporting arrangements may exist to the line manager. The line manager will assess the budget holders performance and will take the appropriate action. Hence, if the budget holder has not undertaken his/her duties to an adequate standard the line manager could reprimand, admonish, or even recommend disciplinary action depending on the nature of the overspending. Conversely, the line manager could praise the budget holder for successful budgetary control and perhaps recommend promotion or some kind of recognition, monetary or otherwise.

Performance appraisal

Many public sector organisations will have utilised some form of performance appraisal system. Such appraisal systems may or may not be linked to pay and benefits and/or promotion prospects. One feature of all performance appraisal systems is the need to assess the appraisee's performance against objectives over a period of time. If budgetary control is a feature of the appraisee's duties, it should be appraised as part of the performance appraisal process and poor performance in this area will result in poor scores, etc.

Service Contract

Many public sector bodies are requiring, either formally or informally, service providers to work under contract. In some cases, service contracts will arise as a result of competitive tendering and in other cases internal service agreements are developed to generate efficiencies in the delivery of service. These arrangements normally set targets for both service delivery and charges. The discipline of working within a contractual framework means that budget holders must keep within budget otherwise the income generated from customers will not cover all the expenditure. In such arrangements the accountability is heightened because any shortfalls that occur due to overspending may result in reduced activity and perhaps redundancies. Obviously the managers of such services are accountable to their colleagues and customers for ensuring services and jobs are maintained.

Pay and benefits

Performance related pay schemes have been introduced in some areas of the public sector. Performance related pay can be structured such that budgetary control success is part of the formula for calculating pay and benefits. One example of this practice is where an organisation sets parameters for budget holders outlining that they must be within, say, 5% of their budget by the year end. If the budget holder failed to achieve these targets then salary increments could be with-held, and in some cases a pay cut could be made. Conversely if the target was exceeded, i.e. savings where in excess of 5%, the budget holder may receive a bonus.

Boards/Committees

In some cases budget holders will be accountable to a board or a committee responsible for overall financial control of the organisation. In particular, budget holders who have overspent will be required to report the reasons for this to the board/committee to whom they will have to account for their financial position. This board/committee will have powers to admonish and discipline if required.

The organisation which implements a devolved budgetary control system should also institute effective methods for accountability. Budget holders should be made aware as to how they are expected to account for their performance with regard to budgetary control.

Summary

☐   In order to ensure budget holders are given the best opportunity to effectively manage their budgets, it is important that management and financial responsibilities are aligned

☐   The involvement of budget holders in budget setting is crucial if they are to be clear about the outputs required. If this is not possible, budget holders should be thoroughly briefed about budgetary expectations

☐   There is a clear link between management and financial responsibility which if not recognised can create problems in budgetary control

☐   One of the keys to successful devolved budgetary control is having an effective process for accountability. This can be achieved through the line manager system, the appraisal system, service contracts, pay benefits or boards/committees

Exercise 13

Being Responsible and Accountable

Scenario A

A training manager is responsible for arranging training courses during the year for a number of departments. Having established what each department requires she then organises the training on their behalf. She is not undertaking any direct delivery herself but is acting as the commissioner of training from external and internal sources. She has arranged for trainers to deliver courses on site; purchased some videos and materials for internal training; and has organised inter departmental training where possible. She has negotiated that each department give her their training budgets to manage in addition to a small centrally held budget. At the end of the year she will have to account both for service delivery and the amounts spent by department. At the moment, although invoices are received for the course materials, trainers, venues etc. and she keeps her own record, she is still unsure as to the real position. Her own records never seems to agree with the computer printouts she receives from the finance department. At the end of the year she has overspent her own budget and when she totals the other departments budgets allocated to her, it is clear that there will also be an overspend of those budgets as well. In order to make the position look better she has been juggling the way in which expenditure has been coded against budgets such that each budget will work out to be only 1% overspent as opposed to some being over and some being under. A 1% overspend on training has been accepted by her line manager. When trying to negotiate for next years programmes she is experiencing disgruntlement from some departments who now say they will not hand over their budgets to her. She does not understand what the problem is.

Scenario B

A legal services section of a local authority are now having to charge all their time on a time recording system so as to adequately assess the cost of each area of work. This will allow them to set up an internal trading account whereby each service is charged for the work undertaken. It has been accepted that there is a need to have a central code for tasks undertaken directly on behalf of the organisation as a whole as opposed to an individual department. There are some departments that require their services on a regular basis such as Social Services, Housing, Land and Properties, etc. and the Legal Services Manager considers that he may be able to introduce a discount system for those departments given the volume of work. Although time sheets have been completed there has not been a distinction between productive time and recoverable time to the client. In some cases it has been necessary to reduce the charge to clients if it is clear that more hours have been charged to the client than should have been necessary for that particular job. The legal service also has to buy in certain services from outside, such as Counsel representation. At present there is no arrangement made as to how this cost is to be covered, and the Legal Services Manager had thought he could absorb this cost in the hourly rates. This has not been the case as Counsel's fees have been tremendous and have been charged to client departments directly, much to the annoyance of those departments who seem to think fees are high due to the poor performance of the Legal Services Department. The legal services manager has collected a lot of data from the time recording system, but still does not know how to charge clients and how to ensure the legal services costs are covered at the end of the year. This year there will be an overspend on budget of 10%.

Consider the two scenarios given and decide in both cases:

a)   who is responsible
b)   who is accountable

for the budgets.

Suggested solutions to this exercise can be found on page 158.

Exercise 14

How responsible and accountable are you?

❖ Given the current climate within your organisation in relation to managing devolved budgets, do you consider that you are responsible and accountable for the budget(s) under your control?

❖ What incentives/penalties are currently in place to ensure that budget holders take their responsibilities seriously?

❖ How do you think your organisation could improve the way in which budget holders are responsible and accountable for their devolved budgets?

Chapter 7

COMMON PROBLEMS IN MANAGING A DEVOLVED BUDGET ANSWERED

In this chapter we set out a number of typical problems that budget holders and managers may encounter in managing a devolved budget, and we suggest answers that may provide a practical way of solving these problems.

> **PROBLEM 1**
> *I manage a budget but do not have the authority required to make the type of changes that I would wish to make to the budget for the good of the service. For example, I cannot use salary budgets to fund other types of goods and services because salaries are ring fenced. Also I cannot change the grades of staff that I manage because the "establishment" is fixed and the personnel department does not allow changes.*

ANSWER 1

It is quite common for public sector organisations to introduce elements of a devolved budgetary system on a stage by stage basis. In some cases this means that the changes necessary for devolvement to work fully have not been made. Ideally, devolvement of budgets also means a devolvement of power to the budget holder, even though many senior managers may wish to retain certain powers. Every organisation will have financial regulations by which they wish to conduct their financial affairs. This may include restrictions such as ring fencing salary budgets. However, given the increasing pressure to reduce public spending and the introduction of competition within the public sector, it is advisable that budget holders have as much flexibility as possible.

It is recommended that budget holders should be able to make virements between salary budgets and other budgets. If the budget holder is to adequately control the service they should be able to have a staffing structure that suits the service even if it means establishment changes. Obviously any changes to staffing would have to be within the context of the organisation's personnel policies.

In order to work successfully within the current regime, the budget holder must clarify what can be done with savings made on salary budgets, i.e. can they be used to support overtime payments, or temporary staff payments, etc. This may provide some flexibility in the way in which human resources can be deployed. The best advice with respect to trying to achieve establishment changes is to lobby the key decision makers in the organisation for change, such that the appropriate decision making power is devolved in line with the budgetary responsibility.

PROBLEM 2
I consider myself to have good budgetary control skills, but I am frustrated in my efforts to manage my budget because half way through the year my budget is often cut without warning or explanation.

ANSWER 2

Everyone in the public sector is aware that budgets are being squeezed at every level. Central government has had a continuing policy to achieve efficiencies in public sector expenditure, and hence efficiency savings have been sought in all areas of public life including the police force, local authorities, education and health authorities. Even if budgets are developed with extreme care, it is difficult to set a perfect budget. Consistent budget management during the ' year is the only way in which an organisation can hope to stay within budget by the year end. One of the actions that arise as a result of budgetary control activities is that budgets may need to be cut in some areas to account for overspending in other areas. Hence, budget holders who may have managed their budgets well during the year may experience cuts for the sake of the organisation as a whole, even though this may seem unfair.

The most frustrating aspect of the current process seems to be the fact that cuts are made without warning and explanation. Budget holders may have to absorb cuts midway through the year which will affect all the existing plans for their service. The reasons for cuts should always be explained, and in order to help with the efficiency of absorbing the cuts, the more notice given the better.

In these cases the budget holder, when informed of the extent of the cuts, needs to re-forecast the whole budget, revise the projected outturn on all budgets and then develop a new plan for the service. The cuts may result in the fact that certain service outputs stated at the beginning of the year can no longer be met. Revisions to service delivery outputs and planned targets need to be made and the relevant senior management of the organisation informed of what the impact of the cuts are going to be. If the budget holder takes this approach, senior management may in some cases reconsider the extent of the cuts if the impact on services is shown to be detrimental.

PROBLEM 3

I have made every effort to be extremely prudent in my expenditure and have created a saving on my budget for the year. However, in my organisation, monies cannot be carried forward to the next year and any savings are used to balance other peoples deficits. I wonder if there is any point in trying to save money if others are to benefit from it.

ANSWER 3

Historically funding has always been established on an annual basis within the public sector. This stems from the fact that government grants and taxes are set annually. At the end of each year, areas of the organisation's spending are consolidated and the overall surplus or deficit achieved by the organisation is carried forward to the following year. These balances are usually referred to as reserves, although there may be other terms used such as general fund, accumulated funds, etc.

Again the good of the whole organisation must come before an individual budget holder's section. Good practice would suggest that budget holders are more incentivised to make savings if they can utilise the savings within their own service area as opposed to the savings being utilised elsewhere. To overcome this dis-satisfaction there are a number of different strategies that can be adopted:

Allow budget holders to keep a percentage of savings ⇨ Allow, say, 50% of savings to be retained by the individual service area with the other 50% going to the general reserves or to fund deficits in other service areas.

Specific developments ⇨ Allow the individual service area making the savings to put forward their future plans for specific developments upon which those savings could be utilised, and then fund according to the organisations priorities.

Trading account ⇨ Allow each service area to operate an individual trading account. Surpluses and deficits will then be carried forward annually. Note: if surpluses are to be carried forward for the benefit of the service, then deficits would also be carried forward to the detriment of the service.

Recognition   ⇨   Budget holders who make savings for the benefit of the organisation could be recognised for their efforts in some formal way even though they are not allowed to keep savings achieved in their area.

PROBLEM 4

I struggle every month to control the budget because the financial management information I receive is very poor. It is out of date, often inaccurate, and very complex to understand. I am aware that it does not show how many invoices are waiting to be paid or my committed expenditure. The financial management report also only gives a cumulative position so I cannot see the individual months transactions. The information never agrees with my manual records therefore I ignore the financial information I receive from the finance department in favour of my spreadsheet figures.

ANSWER 4

Keeping ones own records may help to counter poor financial management information. However, a reconciliation between ones own records and the organisation's financial management information is essential.

Reconciling the manual records to a computerised system, which may be lagging behind, can be time consuming. However, with the aid of a spreadsheet, reconciliations can be performed in a straight forward manner as follows:

Step 1	List actual figures appearing on the financial report produced by the main accounting system.
Step 2	List actual figures as calculated by your locally kept records. These will include commitments and creditors (outstanding bills).
Step 3	Calculate the difference between the two figures. These figures represent the differences that require reconciliation.
Step 4	Identify the reason for the difference in each case. These will usually be timing differences with respect to creditors and commitments. However, they may also be due to error.
Step 5	No action needed if differences are due to timing. If they are due to error, further work needs to be done to identify how the error has occurred and the corrective action taken. This will involve making an adjustment to the main accounts.

Keeping separate records is useful if the quality of the financial information from the main accounting system is not AEIOU (see chapter 5). If local records are being relied upon, it is these actual figures that need to be used when undertaking budget comparisons and implementing budgetary control procedures.

PROBLEM 5

I have given up trying to control my budget because I do not have the time, I do not have any clerical back up or assistants and I do not even have a computer.

ANSWER 5

If the organisation has a strategy of devolved budgetary control, and really believes that this is the most efficient way to control budgets then budget management must be given some priority. Devolvement of budgets requires the budget holder to have additional duties over and above the main focus of their jobs and an allowance needs to be made for this with respect to the allocation of resources. Ideally resources should be devolved along with the budgetary responsibility. In some public sector organisations this has been achieved by devolving central finance officers to departments to assist managers with their devolved budgetary responsibilities.

To undertake the role properly, time needs to be allocated to monitoring and managing budgets. In order to achieve this, one of two things must happen - either the budget holder has to put in additional time (overtime paid or unpaid), or some of the existing duties have to lapse in favour of budget management. The organisation will need to advise budget holders of its priorities so that the budget holder can be effective with regards to their own personal time management.

Devolving budgetary control requires investment in people (training and additional administrative support) and resources (usually technological). If this is not forthcoming then compromises in workloads will have to be made.

PROBLEM 6
At this organisation there has been no financial training or preparation for being a budget holder. No wonder we have all failed miserably and have overspent again as usual.

ANSWER 6

Finance training is essential if an organisation is going to embark on the devolvement of budgets, particularly if it is going to be devolved to levels where a great many staff become budget holders. Due to the technical nature of financial training, it may be an area that cannot be delivered by the in-house training department (if one exists). Occasionally the organisation looks to the finance department to provide the financial training. The difficulty with this approach comes if there is no individual within the finance department with trainer skills, or who wishes to develop trainer skills. The other problem for a finance department is that they will have to identify personnel who will have time to set aside to deliver training programmes. It is for these two reasons why some public sector organisations provide insufficient financial training for budget holders.

Timing of the training is also important. Some organisations have invested a great deal of money in organising financial training well before devolved budgets come into force, only to find that devolvement does not really take place until, say, two years after the training. By this time those who attended the training require refresher courses, and there may be new employees who did not attend the initial training. This would highlight the need to have a continuous rolling programme of financial training, pitched at a number of different levels, to meet the different skills and abilities of the budget holders.

It is possible to obtain training aids, books, etc. to help budget holders with their self development. Although there are many products on the market most are focused on private sector finance and not easily transferable to the public sector.

There are external courses run from time to time, particularly by representative bodies of the sector, and by professional institutes and associations to which public sector employees may belong. For example, courses are sometimes delivered by some public sector unions for the benefit of members and non-members.

If the training within the organisation is insufficient it can be supplemented by external training (although this requires some financial commitment), or a programme of self development using aids such as the books in this series.

PROBLEM 7

I have never been asked about setting the budget although I am expected to control the budget. I don't know where any of the figures came from and they do not relate to the way in which the service is currently being run. For example, some budgets we never use, and other areas are essential but have no budgets allocated to them.

ANSWER 7

The key to effective budgetary control is having a well thought out budget to begin with. It is ideally the role of the budget holder to prepare the budget. In so doing, the budget holder is clear about all the assumptions behind each of the budget headings and how the budgets relate to the way in which the service is to be delivered, and the objectives and targets that should be met during the year.

In some cases it is not practical to have the budget holders prepare the budgets, however, there should be a certain level of consultation. Even if this is not the case, as stated in the question, the budget holder can still be proactive about getting the budget to correctly reflect the service. This can be achieved by following the P.A.T.H.:

Prepare Assumptions that make sense for the current service

    Ask for headings and budgets to be changed as required

        Take positive action to get changes implemented

            Have confidence to redefine the budget within cash limits

When the budget has been redefined to meet the service requirements, the assumptions should be documented such that any new budget holder can understand how the budget has been determined. This approach will require a lot of initial work at the beginning of the year but will make budgetary control for the rest of the year far easier.

PROBLEM 8

I am always told that savings are needed at the beginning of each financial year, but somehow in the last month of the year I am always being requested to spend all this money that has suddenly appeared from nowhere. I know that I often waste the money but I'm told I either spend £x or lose it in next years budget allocation.

ANSWER 8

This problem arises from the same reasons stated in the answer to problem 3. If it is possible to carry forward underspends into a following year, there would be no need to spend up to the limit of the budget each year. If the policy of carrying forward monies from one year to the next is not in place within the organisation, this situation can easily occur. To avoid this happening on a large scale, budgets should be profiled across the year. If they are correctly profiled, underspending can be identified far earlier and appropriate corrective action taken. Ideally, if there are areas where underspends are going to arise, the additional resources that become available should be spent effectively, ideally planned in some way to be spent during the year and not rushed in the last month.

In addition to having budgets profiled, the other effective tool to help identify underspends quickly is to regularly calculate a projected outturn figure either monthly or quarterly. This figure will show if the projected end of year expenditure is below the estimated budget for the year each month/quarter, and hence further planning of expenditure can take place.

PROBLEM 9

How can I control budgets that are uncontrollable. I have to respond to need, just like a fireman I can't let the house burn down because the budget is insufficient to pay staff overtime. As for having to generate an income target - I can't possibly predict how many people are going to buy our information booklets.

ANSWER 9

An uncontrollable budget will still require close monitoring and control. The first element of control is ensuring that there are criteria by which the level of need is determined and that this is monitored closely to ensure that the response given to that need is most appropriate, and the most cost effective. The second element of control is to have a planned level of expenditure based on an estimate of need. This estimate will not be correct because in a demand led service it is impossible to predict the demand, however, the estimate will enable the budget holder to monitor how far away actual demand is from the estimate. Deviations from the estimated demand will have a financial impact and then this can be measured in a planned way. Very high deviations from the initial estimates will mean that there is likely to be overspends. The budget can then be controlled by estimating the extent of the likely overspend and identifying how this can be funded, i.e. where additional funds can be found to meet the overspend.

Estimating demand in a needs led service can only be undertaken by looking at historic trends and trying to establish patterns that can be projected in the future. Even if we take the fire service, they should be able to estimate the average number of call outs per week based on historic experience. They should also be able to estimate the number of call outs that require no action and the number of those that require extensive resources to be deployed. Having worked in an area for a number of years they may also be able to determine which areas within a geographical location are more prone to fires and which times of year fires are more likely to occur; there may be seasonal factors that come into play. Even though each year will be different, there will be a data bank of information that will help to identify whether or not the demand for the service will be very different (higher or lower) from one month to the next and from one year to another. This data can then be fed into the budgetary control system, and budgets adjusted accordingly.

There is no doubt that budgets of a demand led nature within the public sector are difficult to control and do require much more management than budgets for controllable service areas.

Income generated from the general public is also difficult to control. Again this is demand led, because income only arises if the goods and services are demanded by the public and it is difficult to predict how popular certain things are going to be. For example, local authority leisure centres and planning departments are often hit with large fluctuations on income. Unlike the private sector, many public sector services that generate income are restricted. Pricing, for instance, may be dictated by central government, or quango authorities such as pricing regulators. This means that if demand is to fall, there is a limit to how the organisation can respond, i.e. a price increase is not necessarily going to be possible in order to balance the reduced volume; also a price rise may also result in volumes diminishing further. A budget holder with an income budget/target will need to ensure that the budget/target is realistic to begin with taking into account the current market conditions. The budget holder will also need to identify some way of monitoring the factors that affect demand. Where possible, a marketing strategy should also be developed to promote the service and generate more customers.

PROBLEM 10

I am a public servant and not an accountant. I refuse to be held accountable for budgets - its not my job!

ANSWER 10

This is a feeling that has been echoed by many in public service; Doctors, Head Teachers, Social Workers, Civil Servants, Planners, and so on, even the Police Force and Armed forces have been met with budget constraints and stricter accountability. The fact is that the role of a public servant has evolved over the years and now includes an element of financial management and control as well as other aspects of management and service delivery. Most new comers to the public sector are well aware of the importance of achieving value for money and the fact that everyone has to play a role in ensuring budgets are spent as effectively as possible. For some public servants, whose job descriptions did not include this role, there has been a change in culture to which they have had to adjust.

If change is imposed quickly, many people tend to be left behind and feel resentful when it comes to undertaking new duties. The answer is to ensure that everyone participates in the change and can see the relevance of the changes that have to be made to their individual roles as part of the changing organisation. If possible, change should be viewed positively as an opportunity to take a fresh look at things and develop new skills, new techniques, and ultimately better services.

Solutions to Exercises

SOLUTIONS TO EXERCISES

Solution to Exercise 1
Devolvement in Practice

(a) To assist with this solution an organisational chart showing the various levels of responsibility is shown on the next page. Budgets can be split by service area, e.g. Entertainment, and then by activity, e.g. Catering, and then by type, e.g. Food. The number of budget heads will vary depending on the nature and complexity of each service area. Management and financial responsibilities should be aligned. Therefore, whoever is responsible for ordering cleaning materials should have the budget for this spend; in this case the cleaning services manager (or could even be devolved to a lower grade if practical). Similarly the catering manager would have the food purchases budget. These officers are at 4th tier grades in the organisational chart overleaf. Salaries on the other hand may be devolved to head of service or held at a higher level in order to maximise flexibility and control.

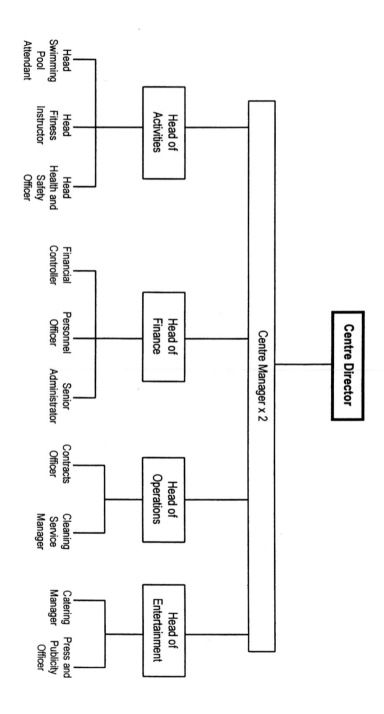

(b) Problems may include:

* *Size of budget (i.e. if it is too large to be effectively managed, or too small to warrant devolvement due to impracticalities)*

* *Complex nature of accounting and reporting*

* *Ability of staff to manage budgets*

* *Increased levels of administration due to the need for increased control checks*

* *Dis-economies of scale*

Solutions may include:

* *Good financial systems which allows for adequate coding and management reports*

* *Training for all staff with budgets*

* *Clear management reporting lines and levels of authority*

* *Regular supervision and review*

* *Continuous independent review of budgets by the head of finance ensure that budgets are devolved where there is a practical benefit, and not just for the sake of devolvement*

Solution to Exercise 3
Developing a Budget from First Principles

a)   Action points should include:

*   *Identifying demand and service level*

*   *Identifying key objectives of the service*

*   *Clarifying the quality criteria required*

*   *Identifying how the service is to be delivered e.g. organisational structure, physical resource requirements etc.*

*   *Identifying how the activity will be funded e.g. public contributions, 100% subsidy or less, grants, etc.*

b)   Typical areas will include salaries, overhead items such as rent, electricity, etc. Sources of information will vary depending on the structure and type of organisation selected. However, it should include written estimates, personnel departments, published data etc., comparisons with other similar organisations, historical information where available.

c)   There is no perfect answer as a number of issues can be debated, however, there should be consistency between the easiest and the most difficult. The difficult areas to budget for are those that will depend on income from the public and are totally demand led such as the leisure centre, as opposed to those that are providing an in-house service such as a personnel department which has relatively fixed budgetary requirements.

An example of a possible ranking is given as follows:

Area	Rank	Reasoning
Quality Assurance Division	1	Fixed service not dependent on volume or selling services.
Contracts Management Unit	2	As above but may depend on the number of contracts to be managed each year.
An Advice Centre	3	As above, but may depend on the number of users.
Personnel Department	4	May have a range of services, some of which may have to be "sold", e.g. training places.
Meals on Wheels	5	Depending on how it is delivered, if under contract may be subject to varying demands on a daily basis.
Secondary School	6	State schools receive formula funding depending on pupil intake number each year which may vary. Private schools depend on fees per pupil and are subject to varying demand and changes throughout the year.
Fire Brigade	7	Due to the nature of the service, volumes cannot be predicted but service has to be delivered on demand regardless of budget implication.
Hospital	8	Similar to above with added complexity if income depends on a number of private beds being sold.
Residential Nursing Home	9	On the assumption that all places have to be sold on the open market without a block contract, there could be a totally variable income throughout the year.
Leisure Centre	10	As above but there is an added complexity given the wide range of activities and services being provided and the wide ranging pricing policy which is normally required.

Solution to Exercise 4
Incremental Budgeting

BUDGET WORKING PAPERS						
Employee Costs						
Name	Basic Salary	Pay Award (note 1)	Total	NI	Pension	Budget
J Brown	40,000	600	40,600	4,243	2,436	47,279
A Taylor	30,000	563	30,563	3,194	1,834	35,591
P Pritkash	22,000	413	22,413	2,342	1,345	26,100
C Doyle	20,000	375	20,375	2,129	1,223	23,727
O Obayo	18,000	203	18,203	1,902	1,092	21,197
D Lincoln	15,000	169	15,169	1,585	910	17,664
R Cohen	13,200	149	13,349	1,395	801	15,545
TOTAL						187,103
Operational Costs						
	Costs Last Year		Inflation			Budget
Transport Costs	10,000		300			10,300
Premises Costs	50,000		1,500			51,500
Supplies and Services	80,000		2,400			82,400
New Developments	0					13,500
Financing Costs	10,000		100			10,100
TOTAL						167,800
TOTAL BUDGET						354,903

Note 1:   Pay award has only a 9 month effect because it begins on 1st July

Solution to Exercise 5
Profiling Budgets

PROFILED BUDGET						
	April	**May**	**June**	**July**	**August**	**Sept.**
Income						
Fees	75,000	75,000	75,000	75,000	75,000	75,000
Total	75,000	75,000	75,000	75,000	75,000	75,000
Expenditure						
Salaries	40,000	40,000	40,000	40,800	40,800	37,740
Central Recharges			20,000			20,000
Supplies and Services	5,000	5,000	5,000	5,000	5,000	5,000
Transport Costs	750	750	750	750	750	750
Professional Fees	10,000	10,000	10,000	10,000	10,000	10,000
Contingency	5,575	5,575	7,575	5,655	5,655	7,349
Total	61,325	61,325	83,325	62,205	62,205	80,839
Surplus/Deficit Month	*13,675*	*13,675*	*-8,325*	*12,795*	*12,795*	*-5,839*

Oct.	Nov.	Dec.	Jan.	Feb.	March	TOTAL
75,000	75,000	75,000	75,000	75,000	75,000	900,000
75,000	75,000	75,000	75,000	75,000	75,000	900,000
37,740	37,740	37,740	37,740	37,740	37,740	465,780
		20,000			20,000	80,000
5,000	5,000	5,000	5,000	5,000	5,000	60,000
2,250	2,250	2,250	2,250	2,250	2,250	18,000
10,000	10,000	10,000	10,000	10,000	10,000	120,000
5,499	5,499	7,499	5,499	5,499	7,499	74,378
60,489	60,489	82,489	60,489	60,489	82,489	818,158
14,511	14,511	-7,489	14,511	14,511	-7,489	81,842

Solution to Exercise 7
Variance Analysis

1.   Interpretation of variances

a)   Overspend of £200 occurring in month 6 assuming previous periods on target

b)   On target

c)   Overspend averaging £200 per month over the last 6 months

d)   Compensating savings made in month 6 to correct previous overspends, cumulative position still in overspend

e)   Overspend in month 6 of £400 reducing previous brought forward underspends resulting in a cumulative overspend of £200

f)   On target for the month but an historic overspend which must have occurred in previous months

g)   Underspend of £200 occurring in month 6 assuming previous periods on target

Information affecting interpretation will include:

- Profile of budget
- Staff numbers and salary levels
- Definition of "salaries" i.e. what is included in this figure
- Activity levels   *

* e.g. (b) appears to be on target but if the budget had been based on 3 employees being in post and only 2 are currently in post then (b) is not on target as one would have expected an underspend on the budget. Variances must be interpreted with supporting management information.

2. Example causes of variances may be:

- Seasonality
- Changes in levels of activity compared to planned activity
- Poor profiling
- Long term sickness
- Inefficiency

3. Examples of uncontrollable variances may be:

- Demands for statutory services
- Changes in legislation e.g. implementation of new health and safety procedures
- Central recharges and allocations

4. Examples of key control mechanisms may be:

- Freeze/reduce expenditure by setting a limit
- Reduce the level of service being provided e.g. opening hours
- Increase income by charging more for services or introducing a charge
- Identify underspent budgets to mitigate overspent ones (Virement)

Solution to Exercise 8
Role of the Budget Holder

a) Steps to be taken from the beginning of the year:

Budget needs to be allocated to each floor/division based on an assessment of need. This should be achieved by initially researching the existing position and establishing furniture requirements for the coming year. Monitoring can then be undertaken on a floor by floor basis.

b) Systems will include:

- Ordering system
- Authorisation process
- Appropriate coding systems such that reports may be generated
- Validation process such that goods received are checked to invoices
- Furniture register/log so that volumes can be monitored
- Preferred supplier lists to enable choice
- Accounting system that generates variance analysis
- Complaints procedure if people are not satisfied

c) Some steps to reduce complaints will include:

- Negotiation and compromise will have to take place in order for the cash limited budget to be divided fairly on a basis of need and for each division to be made aware of their individual budget for furniture. This will enable each division to maintain their own record of purchases if necessary.

- Continued updates should be given to inform divisions of the status of the furniture budget relating to their area.

- The budget split should be re-examined on a regular basis to take account of the current position within each division.

Solution to Exercise 10
Understanding Financial Management Information

a) The initial reaction should be concern given the scale of the unfavourable variances

However, to arrive at a true assessment of the situation, the additional information requested should include:

1. Basis of the budget (budget assumptions)

2. The total budget for the whole year

3. The profiles that have been used

4. The occupancy rates within the school

5. The level of fees being charged

6. The level of outstanding fees to be collected

7. The strategy to raise donations

8. The make up of the other income and strategy to achieve budget

9. What is happening with respect to the recruitment of full time staff

10. Who are the temporary staff and are they in fact covering the vacant posts

11. Current stock levels of the food

12. Details of menus being provided

13. List of equipment being hired

14. Nature of travel and subsistence and staff expenses

15. Plans for purchasing the computer

16. Confirmation that all major repairs are completed

b) Short term actions, largely based upon assumptions made, should include:

* Revising budgets for the second half year based on projected activity to the end of the year; i.e. calculating the projected outturn

* Requesting and receiving the additional information highlighted

* Specific changes to some aspects such as the food purchases, telephone, expenses, the way in which fees are collected, recruitment etc. where stricter control and authorisation procedures should be instituted

* Finance training for the manager and staff

Long term actions, based upon assumptions made, should include:

* Implementation of a marketing strategy if occupancy is a problem

* Implementation of a strict credit control policy if fee collection is a problem

* Review of the school in terms of its long term viability

* Consideration of closure, alternative uses etc.

c) Key management techniques include:

* Communication with all members of staff

* Include staff in decision making process with respect to the formulation of actions to address the position

* Delegate certain budgets to staff so that they are more aware of what is available to spend, e.g. give the catering manager the food budget

* Institute regular reporting mechanisms such that management information is provided on a regular basis

* Institute closer supervision

* Set targets for performance

d)   Key monitoring techniques

    *   Review of financial management information on a regular basis

    *   Review of other management reports such as occupancy and debtors

    *   Regular meetings and progress reports

    *   Regular review of targets against actual performance

	Month 6 Actual £	Month 6 Budgeted £		Projected Outturn £
INCOME:				
Fees	54,000	84,000		108,000
Revenue Grant	20,000	20,000		40,000
Special Grant	30,000	30,000		30,000
Donations	500	1,200		1,000
Other	1,000	12,000		2,000
	105,500	147,200		181,000
EXPENDITURE:				
Salaries	66,000	72,000		132,000
Temp. Salaries	7,000	3,000		14,000
Rent	3,000	3,000		6,000
Gas	1,600	1,800		3,200
Electricity	2,400	2,400		4,800
Telephone	2,100	1,200		4,200
Food	28,000	18,000	(a)	42,000
Equipment Hire	4,800	3,000		9,600
Maintenance	1,000	1,200		2,000
Cleaning	1,100	1,200		2,200
Travel and Subsistence	1,200	600		2,400
Staff Expenses	1,400	600	(b)	1,400
Laundry	1,400	1,200		2,800
Computer	-	10,000	(c)	9,000
Furniture and Equipment	10,000	10,000		10,000
Major Repairs	11,000	10,000		11,000
Sundry	1,800	2,000		3,600
	143,800	141,200		260,200
Recharges	12,500	6,000		25,000
	156,300	147,200		285,200
Overspend	(50,800)			(104,200)

Solution to Exercise 11
Establishing your Financial Management Information Needs

Score the answers given as follows:

(a) 5　　**(b) 4**　　**(c) 3**　　**(d) 2**　　**(e) 1**

Total your combined scores for questions 1 to 10 then read the appropriate summary of your financial information requirements. You may find it useful to evaluate each budget separately if you are responsible for a number of different budgets.

10 - 23

This score would indicate that the budget holder should have a high dependency for comprehensive financial management information. This should include the following:

1. At least monthly, if not weekly financial management reports which show variances for the discrete period and the cumulative period. Variances should be stated both in actual terms and percentage terms. If the system used is a cash accounting system then a list of all commitments (unpaid invoices and orders raised) will also be required and details of accrued expenditure where relevant

2. A monthly revision of the projected outturn based on the most current circumstances and a review of future spending activity for the rest of the year

3. An exception report which picks out major variances and gives detailed explanations of the cause of each variance

4. Access to detailed transactions listings when required

5. On line access to a computerised financial information system

6. An activity report showing levels of service, this may be a time analysis of hours spent, occupancy rates, customer contact numbers, etc. etc.

7. If a staff related budget is one of the budgets under the budget holders control then reports will be required on employee numbers, pay rates, sickness levels, salary enhancements, expense claims, time sheets and so on

8. If income is an area of responsibility then a break down of income sources will be required along with debtors listings etc.

You may be receiving some of this information if not all of it, however, if this information is not being received, you have a financial information requirement.

24 - 37

The budget holder with this score is in a position of requiring regular information which is relatively detailed. The information requirement is not quite as comprehensive as the budget holder that has scored 10 to 23, however, the key reports would include the following:

1. Monthly financial management reports which show variances for the discrete period and the cumulative period. Variances should be stated both in actual terms and percentage terms. If the system used is a cash accounting system then a list of all commitments (unpaid invoices and orders raised) will also be required and details of accrued expenditure where relevant

2. A monthly revision of the projected outturn based on the most current known circumstances and a review of future spending activity for the rest of the year

3. On line access to a computerised financial information system

4. An activity report showing levels of service, this may be a time analysis of hours spent, occupancy rates, customer contact numbers, etc. etc.

5. If a staff related budget is one of the budgets under the budget holders control then reports will be required on employee numbers, pay rates, sickness levels, salary enhancements, expense claims, time sheets and so on

6. If income is an area of responsibility then a break down of income sources will be required along with debtors listings etc.

You may be receiving some of this information if not all of it, however, if this information is not being received you have a financial information requirement.

38 - 50

The Budget holder with this score is in the fortunate position of having budgets that are reasonably stable and easy to control, however they should not be complacent. Even the most straight forward budget still requires monitoring and may sometimes not go according to plan. The financial information required for these budgets include the following:

1. Monthly financial management reports which show variances for the discrete period and the cumulative period. Variances should be stated both in actual terms and percentage terms. If the system used is a cash accounting system then a list of all commitments (unpaid invoices and orders raised) will also be required and details of accrued expenditure where relevant

2. A quarterly revision of the projected outturn based on the most current known circumstances and a review of future spending activity for the rest of the year

3. Occasional activity reports

4. If a staff related budget is one of the budgets under the budget holders control then reports will be required on employee numbers, pay rates, sickness levels, salary enhancements, expense claims, time sheets and so on.

5. If income is an area of responsibility then a break down of income sources will be required along with debtors listings etc.

You may be receiving some of this information if not all of it, however, if this information is not being received you have a financial information requirement.

Solution to Exercise 13
Being Responsible and Accountable

Scenario A

- Training manager responsible and accountable for her own budget

- Other departments responsible and accountable for the budgets delegated to the training manager

- Training manager accountable to the departments

The reason the departments remain responsible and accountable for the budgets given to the training manager, is that she was only "managing" them on their behalf. This means the departments should have been ensuring that they were aware of the status of these budgets at all times and should have taken corrective action when it was clear that they were beginning to become out of control.

Scenario B

- The legal services manager is responsible and accountable for the legal services expenditure budget, and the income budget arising from charges to clients

- As the decision making with respect to instructing Counsel remains in the legal services department it would be appropriate that this budget is also the responsibility of the legal services manager. However, there may be an argument that the legal services manager cannot be accountable for these fees as they are outside of his direct control

Index

INDEX

C

D

E

F

H

I

L

M

N

O

P

R

S

T

U

V

W

Z